What readers are saying about *What Legacy Are We Giving Our Kids?*

Each chapter, in its own way, will facilitate discussion relevant to building positive community within our own families, our cities, and beyond.

> Mary Rice, lawyer, and single mom

Some chapters can help parents teach their children important life lessons and to be more open and respectful as they begin to develop their own understanding of the world.

> Twila, small business owner and mom to a teen and two tweens

This book is upbeat and positive (I chuckled in a few places) even though the subjects are important, necessary, and serious. Oleson encouraged me to think about many things I haven't thought about in years.

> Mary Peterson, preschool teacher for sixteen years

Wow! *What Legacy Are We Giving Our Kids?* is a true gift for Oleson's children and grandchildren.

> Jennifer Malecha, mom to four ages 16 and younger

The stories and examples in Oleson's book trigger the mind to ponder subtle and not so subtle changes in our lives and how they affect our society and our personal lives.

> Darlene Clauson, casual genealogist/historian, great grandma

What Legacy Are We Giving Our Kids?

What
Legacy

Are We Giving Our Kids?

Jon Oleson

Minneapolis

Edited by Jennifer J. Anderson and John R. Kober
Cover design by Robyn Lingen, designwritestudios.com
Interior design by Dorie McClelland, springbookdesign.com
Cover photo by Lara Leimbach, laraphotos.com

ISBN: 978-0-9981785-0-9

10 9 8 7 6 5 4 3 2 1
Printed in the United States of America

The author is donating $2.00 from the sale of each book to effective and
efficient nonprofit programs that 1) help children who need support they
are not adequately receiving, and 2) promote the recovery and sustain-
ability of Earth's physical environment.

Dedication

This book is dedicated to my own kids and grandkids—plus those of everyone else. I also dedicate this book to the many of you who regularly do so much to work for a positive future for all of us, especially our children.

Acknowledgments

I am grateful to Jennifer J. Anderson who worked with me for over a year as I was plugging along with the writing. Her conversations about content and her editing help kept me going in the writing process.

Sincere thanks to my get-it-published team—Dorie McClelland, designer, who two years ago gave me the sense that the book was going to be worth the effort; Robyn Lingen, whose creative work, in collaboration with Dorie, designed an engaging cover; Susan Niemi for helping me connect with the right people and helped me get my head around "doing a book"; and for John Kober who helped me rein in my too free flowing writing instincts so readers wouldn't be thinking "huh?" too often.

How I think and process information has been influenced by my four years at Concordia College (Moorhead, MN) where we were encouraged to be thoughtful and caring. My writing is influenced by English professors Dr. Prausnitz and Dr. Hoppe, and by speech teacher Dr. Dovre.

Thanks also to the many friends and colleagues who supported me in this writing endeavor. My writing and I have been enriched by their participation.

I am forever grateful to my parents and the many people who helped shape my attitudes and character as I grew. Also, I am thankful for the many young children, most of them total strangers, who daily remind me of the importance of writing this book.

Contents

LEGACY: anything handed down from, or as from, an ancestor or predecessor

(Merriam-Webster Dictionary)

Introduction

I am serious when I say I'm not trying to tell anyone what to think. With this book, I am simply writing as an American who works to understand what's going on. I write from my experiences—as a former teacher and administrator, a former small business owner, as a city councilmember, as a member of a faith community, as a dedicated father and grandfather. I write as a fellow American interested in improving the quality and outcomes of dialogue about the state of the country. My goal, in essence, is to promote good conversation.

The idea for this book began several years ago. Like most Americans, I was tired of all the partisan bickering that had dominated Congress for years. Americans were polarizing. I decided to do something about it. I decided to seek a seat in the United States House of Representatives.

Although I didn't really expect to win the election, and I didn't, I did hope to encourage better dialogue—conversation about America, about democracy, core values, leadership, and where we are going. Over the course of my campaign, I was encouraged by the conversation at the hundreds of doors where I was able to engage residents, expressing my concerns and listening to theirs. My belief in Americans was buoyed—we're good people.

I felt better during and immediately after the election. I was less anxious, and the only explanation I came up with was that I was doing something, not just griping. But the ideas and conversations I'd had along the way kept surfacing in my mind. I couldn't think about my grandchildren without wondering, worrying, what their future would be. I decided I needed to try another strategy to move the national dialog in a better direction. The result is the book you hold in your hands.

I write from what I have learned in my lifetime. The chapters that follow cover a sampling of the topics that describe America. They glimpse into the soul of who we are and what we stand for. Some are subtle looks; some are dynamics of America that are loud and in our faces. All require sorting through and taking apart, peeling back of the onion, so to speak, so we can see what's at the core.

Who do I want to read this book? Anyone who wants to

- step away from the hectic pace of life in America to reflect about life and what's most important,
- step away from the confusing, often disturbing way America "does politics," and
- participate in shaping America's future.

The stories that launch most chapters are in this book because they have helped me get my head and heart around issues and the people dynamics that affect America's ability to understand how we best govern our nation, how we make interactions between us more effective, more productive.

My stories and my processing how they relate to America help me understand all this. They're my perceptions, my takeaways. I offer them fully expecting that readers will be in sync with some chapters, dismayed or repulsed by some, bored by others. My hope is that this book will provoke interesting and helpful thinking and dialog. It is my expectation that you will resolve to increase your engagement in America's future, deciding that you can make a difference. It is my hope that you will do your part to stop the squabbling we hear every day, that you will actively support good problem solving and good future planning.

This book puts thoughts on the table for you to consider. To ponder. To stir up your creative thinking. To do some self-examination. It is my hope that you will do your own analysis of what America values and who we want to be as a nation, as a world leader. It is my firm belief that we share similar thoughts about what we want the American experience to be for our kids and grandkids.

Chapter 1

Chip Off the Ol' Block

**We are shaped by others at least
as much as we shape ourselves.**

It's amazing how many of the expressions I heard as a child have stayed with me—and probably influenced me more than I've realized. I overheard someone say, "He's a chip off the old block," at a social event recently. It is not something one hears on a regular basis, so I guess I thought the phrase had died out. It still doesn't make literal sense to me. Perhaps my understanding of it as a kid still works today: *the guy described is a lot like his dad.*

That meaning fits my relationship with Dad in quite a few ways. I can trace quite a few of my characteristics to him. Parents (Mom is part of me too!) generally interact with us more than anyone else when we're children, so it makes sense that they influence and shape who we evolve into as adults. Fact is that a lot of people influence us in big and little ways throughout our lives. We're chips off of many blocks.

The "Chip off . . ." comment flashes me back to my childhood. I recall some adults who complemented my parent's influence by being role models, offering helpful comments, and simply caring for me. There was my Boy Scout leader, John Sulerud. Elder Aalgaard, who took me fishing with his son, and my friend Bruce. My high school English teacher, Helen Sjolander. A potato farmer, Bennett Aarestad, who hired me for four high-school summers and often invited me to join his family at their lake cabin for summer fun. Even cameo players like Johnny Johnson, a neighbor across the alley, who gently pointed out one summer day that I should be a gentleman and use the harder-to-pull garden rake and let my sister use the easier, springy rake.

I reflect more now about the relationship I had with my father than before he died in 1999. I catch myself doing something or saying something that reminds me of him, such as digging tree leaves into my garden each fall to refresh soil nutrients and to better hold moisture for plants. Or beveling the snow along sidewalks and driveway when I shovel. I recall hearing, "It looks better and it's less likely you'll knock snow into your boots as you walk near it."

My sense of humor is a lot like his. Too often I draw on some of his corny comments, like saying "Peas to meet you" when passing the peas at dinner. But I, perhaps like Dad, discovered how valuable it is to laugh and how much people generally appreciate getting the lift in life that a little humor can produce.

How much have I copied my dad? Hard to know. What I do know is that I observed Dad modeling many positive traits. My dad was a hard worker, very responsible, took life pretty seriously. The fact that he served as a pastor in his era probably had a lot to do with that. Pastors were looked up to—and watched closely. Any social impropriety by him (or me!)

would lead to gossip around the small towns he served. No bad language, don't speak ill of anybody, don't speed, raise perfect kids. A lot of do's and don'ts. I think about those standards almost like he and Mom are still looking over my shoulder.

Dads (and moms) model simply by being in their kids' lives. I was fortunate in having a dad who was home and involved in my life a lot during my formative years. He was around for me to watch; I heard him philosophize; I heard him make comments about events. I was on the receiving end of his efforts to get me to think about and assimilate good values.

I was learning pretty straightforward stuff about how humans develop. Straightforward but typically overlooked. I didn't think about such things as I developed into a young adult. In fact—call me a slow learner—it was only recently that it dawned on me how much I was shaped by my parents and others.

My reflecting about how much others influenced who I am today has resulted in three main takeaways. First, it's a bit unnerving to realize how much I was shaped. I didn't create my own life as much as I thoughtlessly assumed. I'm amazed that a thinker like me didn't realize what was happening until decades later.

The second takeaway follows naturally from the first: the shaping process happens subtly. The memories that now explain where I got some of my traits are merely the tip of the influence iceberg. When Mr. Aalgaard took me fishing he gave of his time, skills, and attitudes. In doing so he modeled important values, including helping with a task, sharing knowledge, including others in what you do, and being patient. When Mrs. Sjolander managed her classroom she encouraged and challenged us to learn well, to learn the self-discipline it takes to understand and gain skills you don't yet know you need, and to learn the value of taking pride in producing quality work.

> *Influence Takeaways*
> *1. Others shape us.*
> *2. Process is subtle.*
> *3. Keep eyes open.*

Takeaway number three is that I wish I had been more conscious about the process so I could have been a bit more choosey in which influences I let mold me. Don't get me wrong, I benefited from a lot of good modeling from parents and others. It's just that I wasn't eyes wide open. It's that I would have, for example, worked to achieve better balance in work and play. I would have gone fishin' more, stayed in adult sports leagues longer, hung out with the guys more.

It's not that parents and others who influenced me tricked me. Far from it. Sure, it's a parent's job to train children in the way they should be, but I was never forced to live like them my whole life. Much of their influence happened simply by living their lives in my presence. It's on me that I didn't schedule pauses amidst the hectic life to reflect about what was happening. I realize now how valuable that would have been.

My life now is at high noon. Well, maybe more like 5:00 p.m. Twilight is on the horizon. But there's still time for me to pause and consider redirecting who I am a little, to be more self-designing. I'm working on that. We can all relish in the traits we like about ourselves, however we got them. And we can work to modify, reshape the traits that aren't working so well for us.

But I'm also trying to figure out how to pass on my three takeaways to my kids and, in more simplified ways, to my grandchildren. We can't back up all of our lives to do something differently. I feel good about some of the traits they may have "inherited" from me. For others, I wish I had "fixed me" before they were toddlers. My aim is to strike a balance between alerting them to the subtle yet very powerful ways we humans are shaped—our values, personality traits, and lifestyles—and "letting them" experience and discover the influencing process on their own.

A parent's influence—any influence that shapes us into who we become—should not simply be thoughtlessly adopted. The "evolving me" benefits from regular review. In the end, we need to be more than the sum of the chips off the ol' blocks.

Q*s*

1. What general kinds of help might a young male need to realize how his dad influenced him? Who, if anyone, "has the right" to help another person, of any age, decide which influences are good and which are not?

2. Does the chip off the ol' block dynamic happen differently in a mom-daughter relationship?

3. Too many kids do not have both parents, or even one, providing positive life shaping influences during their young, very formative years. Do our communities offer significant and ethical backup influences that are positive?

4. Who do you influence and what is the result?

Chapter 2

Learning from Chickens

**How do we move away from squabbles to skilled,
thoughtful problem solving?**

"Hobby farms are a great place to raise children." That's what we thought in the early 1970s when my first wife and I bought a twenty-acre portion of a former dairy and raspberry farm a few miles North of Duluth, Minnesota. We weren't disappointed.

The kids learned a lot about the great outdoors—lots of opportunity to explore nature as part of play and quiet time. It was a great place for us to teach and for the family to learn the responsibility side that accompanied the fun side of raising rabbits, having a horse, and eating our own farm fresh eggs.

I of course had the adult's share of baling hay, caring for the feeder steer, and other physical work, including building a chicken netting fence to keep predators from reducing our small flock. I loved all of that.

Some of our farm animals frustrated me on occasion, like the habit our mare had of grazing in our back yard when she discovered the electric fence had shorted out. But on balance our backyard critters gave us a lot of positives, including wholesome food and unusual lessons about almost any facet of life.

I got one of those lessons one day as I approached the chicken coop to look for eggs. Two young roosters, almost old enough to become fryers in our freezer, were having some kind of disagreement. They'd jump at each other, wings flapping and beaks jabbing, then back up and start all over again. I stopped to watch.

Their conflict evolved into a head to head standoff as they appeared to be doing a comically strange dance. Foreheads nearly touching, their heads bobbed up and down in perfect sync. Just then another chicken approached and walked right between them. I have no idea why. It was a simple action, the chicken simply going about her business of getting "over there" in the quickest way, I guess.

The two young roosters, their fight disrupted, both wandered off. It was the strangest thing! One moment going at each other, the next moving on with chicken life, as though there had never been a problem.

Decades later, this imagery came back to me as I became increasingly frustrated by the squabbles I consistently observe in American society. I decided America needs a chicken to walk through the roosters—the humans who are flying into each other's faces with emotion wings flapping, harmful words jabbing, and stare-offs like those two roosters were doing. America needs to *restart* how we get along, especially in how we govern ourselves.

Governing ourselves? Why, that's us! It's our responsibility as individuals to reset how we get along, it's us who need to walk between the squabblers and get them to stop the standoffs, the political bickering, and get back to making America work as united states. We can do that.

Why do humans squabble? Answering that question is more than I can handle. But I've lived such an experience-rich life that I can talk about plenty of examples of how we don't get along, as well as how we do. I've watched us, felt myself, squabble about issues. I've observed others, participated in, relationship problems that clearly happened because we're all unique. Sometimes we don't understand each other, don't communicate well.

Can we accomplish what that chicken did when she walked between the two roosters that were arguing? It's clear that America needs to stop the unproductive bickering, clear our heads, and start afresh. The partisan and polarizing behaviors that dominate American life today are poisoning our way of life.

We need to get to skilled, thoughtful problem solving. We need to get to skilled, thoughtful planning. Problem solving and planning the future are critically important elements that must be accomplished well for any community, any nation, to succeed and thrive. Problem solving and planning in a democracy requires teamwork attitudes and behaviors.

We aren't chickens. We may not dare walk between people who are shouting philosophical differences. But each one of us can—must—do our part to move the United States of America toward a more productive, harmonious future.

Fortunately America is blessed with resources to help us work through and work out of the squabbles that so tragically divide us. All we need to do is see, admire, and be inspired by the many good examples going on right in front of our eyes.

Q_s

1. What prompts you to think about the issues and dynamics facing America?

2. What can you do as an individual, or as part of a group, to engage in the work that is necessary for productive problem solving and planning to happen?

3. When have you needed to be the "chicken" that walks between the "roosters"?

4. What good examples have you seen of people ending squabbles and getting along in your community, in our country?

Chapter 3

Research Papers and Prairie Dogs

**Finding good information and seeing
the big pictures of life are important.**

It was during the 1988-89 school year at the University of
Arizona that I couldn't take it anymore. I had taken a one-year
leave from teaching to pursue a graduate school degree, and
the superintendent class I registered to take that spring called
for a research paper as a major requirement. The dread of
doing yet another one was so overwhelming that I set up an
appointment with the professor.

My thoughts were organized as I strode into his office. "Dr.
Grant, I need to request an option to doing the research paper
requirement for your grad level class. I've done many. It's true
they've helped me find facts and quotations I can weave into
professional papers, but I believe I'll benefit more from an
option I'm proposing."

I went on to say I knew there were lots of issues a public
schools superintendent needed to address—class size, school
boundaries, teacher and administrator skill sets, parent relations, budget, job descriptions, facilities management, and a
number of other issues and dynamics. I wanted to devise a

plan that would help me collaborate with *my* school board and department heads so we all understood how the specific issues I wanted to work on fit into the context of the our unique school district.

I told Dr. Grant I wanted to get my head around a *process;* I wanted to learn how to scope out an issue so I'd be better able to manage school district problem solving and strategic planning. I told him I believed the paper I was proposing would help me do that.

I took the class in case I should choose to steer my educator career into school district administration. I knew that, if I became a superintendent, I would want to address district needs by seeking to understand the big picture of school district dynamics. This would set the stage for my pulling together a diverse district team, which was my leadership style, to develop a shared vision of what we wanted to accomplish. The paper I proposed would conceptualize one focused issue that districts could reasonably expect to face. In effect this would be a practice run at a process that would prepare me for an actual scenario later.

He bought it! He knew I would not be going to the research library—there would be few if any footnotes in the paper. He knew I'd be drawing on my own experience and initiating conversation with others, people in the Tucson schools where I was interning.

I called the project The Affective Reading Program (TARP). My goal was to conceptualize how I could guide my district through a process that would take a fresh look at how we help students learn to read. Learning is more than simply a cognitive process, and I knew it would be helpful to better understand how student feelings relate to the dynamic process of learning to read.

My paper got done. It turned out to be a lot harder to do than the research paper I managed to avoid. But the whole process helped me get a better feel of how I'd approach needs in a school district. It helped me think about *big pictures*, helping me see how the very issues on which research papers narrowly focus interconnect with other issues.

I never put these outcomes to use as a superintendent because I never pursued that career; however, the process of scoping out the importance of getting a big picture understanding about pretty much anything has been invaluable to me. Working to understand big pictures, seeing how interrelated things are in daily life, has been very helpful to me personally. I believe I experience fewer bad surprises, discover fewer unintended negative consequences from decisions I make, and generally live a smoother life.

I work harder now to understand people and events in their contexts. Each event involves human actors that shape its direction. Each individual has his or her own DNA, personality and life experiences. Each event exists in a web of other events that affect it.

I picked up another very valuable life guide while driving in part of America's vast prairies in April, 2009. This second "out West" experience, hundreds of miles north of Arizona, became an important complement to my university "the importance of understanding the big picture" experience. The prairie helped me understand how difficult it is to see some parts of the big picture.

While driving along a remote Wyoming stretch of roadway, I noticed quick movements of small creatures on the landscape. I slowed down and discovered a village of prairie dogs. I stopped to turn around and go back.

I watched from the car for a while and then got out. I slowly walked closer to some of the holes on the edge of the vast community. The dogs continued doing their "now you see me, now you don't" routines. For a while I focused on just one hole. The dogs going in and out were different sizes.

I drew a tentative conclusion that there was either a family who called a particular hole its own, or there was a tunnel system underground with the surface holes actually community use features leading to streets going to multiple family dens. The longer I watched and thought though my hypothesis, the more I realized my tentative conclusion about their family dwellings was in need of knowing a lot more about prairie dogs and their environment.

I headed back to my car and resumed my journey. Many miles of lonely driving on good roadway gave me lots of thinking time. Seeing for myself would be a great way to find answers to my basic prairie dog questions, but I was too big to fit in the holes. Even if I could fit, I couldn't shake the scary thought that I didn't have enough information about prairie dogs to know if I'd be welcomed or bit!

A few more miles down the road I realized my twenty minutes of watching prairie dogs didn't even tell me whether they lived as family units, much less whether or not they lived in tightly knit family-type groups. Maybe they went down the nearest hole and slept wherever they happened to be when they got sleepy. I chose to be content with musing about how biologists would maybe get good information about prairie dogs.

I learned very little about prairie dogs that day, but the roadside experience did become an important life guide for me. That stop reminded me how important it is to look beyond the readily apparent. There is knowledge, awareness, and insights in *tunnels*, in places we don't naturally look. Understanding what happens in the parts of the world that are not readily perceived can be, and often is, critically important.

A personal goal formed in my life that day on that quiet Wyoming road. I decided I need to work at being more curious, more humble, and more determined to explore my unknowns, to work to understand what I don't understand. I need to seek good information even when it is tunneled out of ready sight.

There is a human impulse to stay in comfort zones, to put up walls of all sorts around us so we aren't confused by too much information, unsettled when hearing the opinions and beliefs of others that differ from the beliefs and opinions to which we've become attached. I can't simply curl up in the mental-emotional fetal position I sometimes want to retreat to when life seems too complex.

I understand all that, feel it often. But I know I make better decisions when I take the time and make the effort to explore what's underground, to seek what's not readily apparent.

Two out-west experiences led to two excellent life lessons. *Seeing the big pictures of life is important.* It's a great personal life skill, a helpful attitude. We also need to understand the interconnectedness of life on behalf of our nation. That lesson needs to align with the second lesson I learned on that trip. *Finding good information is important.* We need to look for good information wherever it may be. It takes time and effort but there's something very cool about finding something that others tend to miss.

Q_s

1. What "information in tunnels" have you discovered that especially helps you in life?

2. "Out of sight, out of mind" is a simple comment about a huge reality. "What we don't know can hurt us" is another. Is there an issue America faces today that especially needs to be examined with these warnings in mind?

3. How would you rate how good Americans are at grasping big pictures and seeking out good information?

4. How are our government leaders doing? Do they make genuine, thoughtful efforts to understand big pictures and ferret out good information as they problem solve and strategize a good future for America?

Chapter 4

Patriotism

**Broaden your actions to show patriotic support
of the United States.**

Talk about patriotism comes up frequently in the American
political arena. Too often I get the feeling that politicians
use the term to try to convince voters they're more patriotic
than their opponents, that their party is more patriotic than
the other party. We need to broaden our understanding and
expression of the concept because it's central to securing
America's future.

One of the more common contexts in which Americans talk
about patriotism is when we express support of our military
service men and women. Acknowledging and showing appreciation for those who disrupt their lives and risk death is very
important. Honoring those who serve in our armed forces
acknowledges the benefits all Americans get when young men
and women put their lives on the line to defend our nation. It
is good; it is patriotic to do so.

One particular experience illustrated for me how important it
is to show such appreciation in a genuinely sincere way. I met an
elderly relative for the first time at a family reunion some twenty

years ago. Conversation revealed that he had served America in World War II. I thanked him for his service and noted the sacrifices he and his family experienced. He was clearly moved by my expression of thanks, and I vowed to make a point of thanking veterans and those currently serving whenever I discovered their service status.

A common display of patriotism that goes beyond words is wearing a United States flag pin. For a while after the terror attacks of September 11, 2001, the pin became almost a literal requirement among politicians in Washington, DC and beyond. Some, like my wife and I, fly the flag in our yard. Bumper stickers, attending Memorial Day and 4th of July events, and specific clothing declare "I am patriotic."

It's very appropriate and important to be patriotic in these ways, but if that's all we do, it's not enough. We need to broaden our actions to show patriotic support of the United States. The samples below list some ways, their variety suggests there are more.

- It's patriotic to do the things that improve our personal health. It's good for us as individuals and it's good for our nation when we don't claim unnecessary health care expenses. Both actions reduce workplace insurance costs or reduce Medicare and Medicaid costs.

- It's patriotic to put in an honest day's work at whatever level of a business, or non-profit, or governmental organization that gives us a pay check. Every honest worker helps our nation compete internationally.

- It's patriotic to pay taxes, and it's patriotic to expect that governmental revenues are spent wisely.

- It's patriotic to assist individuals within our communities who need a helping hand—whether the need stems from a personal crisis (for example, extended illness or severe accident or injury) or a large-scale disaster (events like Katrina, 9/11, tornados).

- It's patriotic for us to support ourselves just as much as we are able, so we don't place unnecessary burdens on our families, community, state, and nation.

- It's patriotic for businesses to charge customers (including the government) reasonable rates above real costs.

- It's patriotic to dialog with an open mind even when we don't agree with someone else's position.

- It's patriotic to work toward consensus, realizing that nations can be destroyed from within when partisan divisiveness replaces consensus building as the norm.

The United States of America, like any nation, needs a feeling of cohesion, a feeling that we are best off when we work together and support each other. Our military service men and women certainly deserve our support. Wearing American flag pins, attending Memorial Day and 4th of July events, and waving the American flag are patriotic actions. But our patriotism is most powerful when we also live our lives, every day, in ways that help our nation succeed.

*Q*ₛ

1. What does "being patriotic" mean to you?

2. The bulleted comments above make a point that true patriotism requires us to match what we say with nation-supporting actions. How patriotic are Americans today?

3. It's human nature to want what's good for us as individuals. What motivates you to do what's best for the nation even when it doesn't seem like it's best for "me"?

Chapter 5

Burned Bacon Days

**Bad days happen—being up-front about them
can improve your mood.**

I'd been teaching a couple years when I got a lesson in just
how much humans are affected by how their day is going. My
students at the time were seventh, eighth, and ninth graders,
the fun range of years when the transition to adolescence is in
active mode. Some teens are very direct, less encumbered by
political correctness than their elders. It was that sometimes
bold openness that triggered a good lesson for me.

This you-can-learn-a-lot-from-an-adolescent experience
started to roll when a still somewhat meek seventh grader
asked me a question as she left class one day. "Mr. Oleson,
are you having a bad day?" I'm sure my defense mechanism leaped into action to protect my self-image. I probably
(instinctively) told her, "No," followed by "Why do you ask?"
I don't remember the conversation well, but I clearly recall
that her comment got me thinking.

I reflected about *bad day* dynamics over the next few days.
I started by thinking that, yes, bad days happen and many
things can trigger them. The young girl's comment really
pushed me to better understand how my bad days affected

students since there's a tendency for many of us to be unaware of how we come across to others. As a teacher I realized I really needed to understand how my bad days impacted classroom dynamics, how I affected thirty or so kids forced to be in my charge for class time.

A teacher having a bad day is bound to affect many aspects of a classroom: student attitudes about adults, the willingness to get involved in classroom activities, and the amount of learning going on. Sometimes bad days can get contagious and, trust me, you don't want thirty some adolescents holed up in one room to all get irritable.

My reflecting on the incident prepared me to talk to my class the next time I realized I was having a bad day. Driving to school one morning after a slushy snowfall gave me the opening I wanted. I told my students at the beginning of first period that I was having a bad day. Bad roads, some lousy drivers, and getting to school late had me tensed up. I knew I was irritable. I asked them to cut me a little slack that day: no goofing around, being sure to follow directions, and stuff like that.

Remembering that adolescents tend to have a hypersensitivity to fairness, I thought it wise to tell them that I would try to go easy on them when they were having a bad day. I gave them the option of letting me know as they came into class on a bad day. It was their choice if they wanted to tell me why. Somehow I realized that what I'd just said could get out of hand. So I went on to say I'd get suspicious if a kid told me on a regular basis he or she was having a bad day. A couple kids did little laughs and soon a couple more laughed. The whole class probably imagined which jokesters or which slackers might try to take advantage of my offer.

Those couple of minutes did some wonderful things for me and, ultimately, for my classes from then on. Being upfront with them about having a bad day actually put me in a better mood. A benefit to me. But we all benefited in another way. Our relationship moved to being less distant. By telling students that I wasn't on top of everything, I was letting them know that teachers are human too, and we care about how we make students feel.

My students realized schools weren't so much us (kids) and them (adults) and that we were somehow in this school business together, in the same boat so to speak.

I realized my students were attentive and seemed to appreciate the thoughts and ideas that spilled out of me. The discussion went on a bit as we exchanged examples of the variety of things that can cause bad days.

I suggested we call bad days *burned bacon days.* Bacon, in those days, was a breakfast thing, and bad days often started early. Burning the bacon would definitely be a bad start to a day, so I told them we could use burned bacon day as code for "I'm having a bad day."

The name stuck. Over the next several weeks we put the idea into effect, and "I'm having a burned bacon day" became shorthand for "go as easy on me as you can." Some of my classes really got into it; others not so much, but I realized the idea spawned by that uninhibited seventh grade girl's "Mr. Oleson, are you having a bad day?" was making me a better teacher.

A simple process to handle an ordinary thorn in life was born that slushy, snowy day. It ended up having some neat outcomes, which I didn't anticipate as I started that class period. All of us, me as teacher and the kids as students, discovered that simply telling someone how we're feeling—that we're having a bad day—can be therapeutic. We often feel better when we share that kind of news.

After that experience, I started each new class every semester with a "Burned Bacon Day" section in my classroom procedures handout. I believe my ability to relate to my students went up a notch for the rest of my career.

Perhaps everyone has had a light bulb turn on in some situation, an enlightenment that gives ideas about how to get along better with others. My example showed me how expressing empathy for someone pays dividends for those on the receiving end as well as for those showing empathy. It's actually quite logical. We naturally go easy on a person having a bad day because we are fully aware that we all have had, and will continue to have, bad days. Part of leaving a legacy to young people can be as simple as passing on such personal *aha* experiences.

What goes around comes around. You scratch my back and I'll scratch yours. Do for others what you'd like them to do for you. Phrases like these indicate to me that our ancestors—people in any culture—have found how valuable it is to leave the legacy of helping others when they're having bad days.

I'm glad that seventh grade girl was willing to ask me if I was having a bad day. She helped me focus on an important dynamic that I needed to get my head around to better manage my classroom. That focus has helped me develop better relationships with people throughout my life.

Imagine what life in America would be like if we all helped each other get through burned bacon days.

Q_s

1. In what contexts, besides schools, do we need others to cut us some slack?

2. Do you find the benefits you receive when showing empathy are greatest with any particular type of person?

3. How do you motivate yourself to show empathy to someone you realize needs it but for some reason repels you, perhaps because he or she is obnoxious, ill kept, or has some other trait that turns you off?

4. Are there times when empathy is more effective when delivered without words, through a look, the sound of your voice, or some other nonverbal expression?

Chapter 6

Wrinkles: They're Only Skin Deep

What diverse factors go into making a person a person?

The face I saw in the mirror while washing my hands at the Shantytown burger place in my neighborhood startled me a bit. I saw some skin sags under my chin that I hadn't noticed before. To make matters worse, some wrinkles seemed more pronounced. "I'm not forty anymore!" I thought.

Since starting this book several years ago, I have developed a habit of jotting down thoughts while they're fresh in my mind. This time I had no paper on me so I asked my waitress. "That'll do. Thanks!" I said as she gave me a couple sheets from her order form pad.

My first thought as I settled in to wait for my burger was, "At least my grandkids seem to like me!" I couldn't help but smile as lots of images flashed into mind: Bringing then four-year-old Ian to Lake Harriet so he could catch and release sunies and bluegills; baseball game picnics for combined birthday parties for Kate and Jeremiah; the poem Sophi wrote about me, framed, and gave to me on my sixty-eighth birthday; wearing myself out as I played sports in Jack and Brady's basement; times when a grandkid came into the house, didn't see me right away, and asked "Where's Grandpa?" I recalled the summer hours when I could just hang out with Florida and Minnesota grandkids as they played on the swings, monkey bars, and other fun things at Valley View playground.

This reminiscing exercise calmed and soothed my mind. "I'm more than wrinkles," I thought. I started to feel better; the images with grandchildren buoyed my spirit. I would have gone back to watching a game on the restaurant TV but the mirror and grand-kid memories were too powerful, and I had to figure out who I was besides being an older guy with wrinkles and sags.

I philosophized. How big a deal is it to have wrinkles, one of the classic indicators of aging? Who cares? Maybe I should see them as a badge of honor, take the offensive! My grandchildren don't seem to notice, or at least don't seem to care, that I am getting sags and wrinkles. What *do* they see in me that draws us into a loving, care-about-each-other relationship?

A good relationship doesn't develop if it stays at a shallow, inadequate level. Moving to a deeper relationship requires a lot of thinking about stuff we don't typically think about. We do better when we think about our relationships. It helped me, for example, when I recalled that it was a host of common interests that drew childhood friend Buppy and me into a friendship. It helps to understand why friends continue to like each other even when a disagreement strains the relationship.

My burger and a second beer arrived. As I began to eat, my mind shifted to thoughts about funerals. Yes, funerals. I wasn't leaping from wrinkles to thoughts that I was about to kick the bucket. No, I thought about some of the couple dozen memorial services I've attended. My sister Rhoda died from Leukemia at age four, giving me, at the tender mind and feeling age of six, my first big jolt of what death meant. There have been many more. A nineteen-year-old neighbor kid, a fellow educator, parents, aunts, and uncles died at different stages of their lives. Death has a way of getting us to think beyond wrinkles as we do our life expectancy math.

I believe all of the eulogies and conversations before and after the funerals that I've attended focused on the deeper side of whom each of these friends, colleagues, and relatives were. We don't focus on the skin deep stuff. We don't talk about wrinkles and sagging skin. At most we talk in passing about what they looked like. On the other hand we hush up, perhaps get emotional, as family members and close friends talk about what they will most miss about the deceased. We tell stories that describe what made them special to us, what made them a person and not just another human being.

As we interact with people during our lifetimes, our brains subconsciously process how animated they are, how happy or sad they are, how articulate they are. As we get to know them better, we come to understand the *why's* of their animated, happy, and sad times. We discover (especially if we ask) what motivates them to speak clearly and with understanding about some topics. A whole range of inputs tell us a lot about who each one is as a person.

My burger, fries, and a beer now long gone, I realized that the simple act of looking into that mirror while washing my hands had prompted a lot of mind wondering. I think the result was thought therapy that helped me recover from a reality shock. All the mental noodling and time with wide-ranging memories did the job. The bottom line is that I am more than a body. Getting wrinkles isn't so significant. If others take the time to know me, they will ultimately like me or reject me because of what's on the inside, not the outside.

I was content to walk out of the hamburger place without a complete answer to what it means to be a person. I was reminded that when it comes down to what's really important, it's the stuff beyond my physical being that makes me who I am. It's my habits, tendencies, idiosyncrasies, how I interact with people, and the things I do that make others smile or frown. Such descriptions of any one of us resonate somehow in others who know us. It's these thoughts that echo within us long after family and friends, and even lesser-known acquaintances, have passed on.

I decided before I got home from my burger run to think of my wrinkles and sags with a level of pride! I don't need to get my sagging skin tucked, or whatever they do nowadays. Wrinkles go with age and you can't have real wisdom until a body has lived this long!

Q*s*

1. Think for five minutes about a very good friend. Why are you friends?

2. As you think about your friends, do you find that opposites, in fact, do attract? Why do opposites sometimes become such good friends?

3. What characteristics of people you cared about and loved during their lifetimes linger in your mind as memories?

4. What makes a person a person?

Chapter 7

Ankle Bone Connected to the Pituitary Gland (What??)

**We are all unique and require
inquiring health-care minds.**

A high school music teacher introduced me to a catchy spiritual/folk/gospel song about how human bones connect. The song returned to mind as I envisioned this chapter. I web-searched for the name because memory only served me a garbled recollection of phrases. Although there seems to be agreement that the words come from the book of Ezekiel in the Bible, it turns out both the title and the words vary according to source. Perhaps that gives me poetic license to connect the song to health care in America.

The human body is an amazingly complex, integrated, and fine-tuned phenomenon. Unfortunately the brand of medicine that dominates American health care doesn't act like it knows that. We are bones and organs and connective tissue and protective systems and chemicals and an amazing internal communication system. We're served by medical professionals who see component parts and go about their business via focused diagnosis and prescriptive treatment perspectives.

I must quickly go on to say two things. The medical professionals who have, and still do, care for me are very professional and want to help me be healthy in both preventive and fix-me ways. They care. The other important background to this chapter is that I'm an outlier—someone who doesn't fit a mold—so my story is unique. Or is it? Readers may find some parallels to their situations, or not.

One of the team at a wound clinic who genuinely worked hard to heal chronic sores on the sides of my feet/ankle areas commented, with a mix of concern and a smile in her voice, "You're complicated." She knew my history. Phlebitis in one leg as a high school junior and in the second leg as a college freshman. Ulcerative colitis diagnosed at age 23, treated ever since. All but fifteen centimeters of colon removed in 2008, and doctor disagreement if the rest should now be removed.

Some doctors say the colitis and sores are directly related, others say there isn't a connection and the sores are totally circulation related. I say there's more to explain my daily GI tract problems and sores problems than what any of the forty-some years of doctoring ever considered.

All of us are medically unique. I get that. It doesn't seem that American doctors are given the time and the freedom and rewards in their institutionalized system to treat us as unique. Each human gets different DNA and a mess of other pass-downs from relatives. Each of us eat, drink, breath different stuff. We have different pH levels, different chemical makeups. We react to doctor prescriptions differently, just as we do to eye liner, genetically modified foods, fragrances, food types, too little sleep, and stress. We take care of ourselves differently. I get it that being an effective, helpful doctor is not easy.

I'm not trained in medicine in a professional sense. However, I do have training from the "school of hard knocks." We all attend that school. Our learning opportunities occur as we visit doctors, get surgeries, and consider the home remedies and folk medicine passed on from our families and friends. Each of us has the opportunity to think about, observe, and learn from personal experiences that include lots of trial and error learning.

I've learned a lot about the human body and how to care for it from a variety of sources. I've needed to check out options because the dominant medical systems in America haven't figured out the unique combination of major health issues I have. I first heard about the reason it's good to know about human body pH levels from the man who replaced my shower floor tiles. I benefit from my chiropractor's periodic suggestions. Dr. Jennifer's suggestions that I try going without wheat for thirty days and sip water diluted with high quality apple cider vinegar were spot on. Family stories led me to discover that my body responds better to aloe vera than Rx antibiotics. A clinical nutrition professional told me (later confirmed by my regular doctor) that managing inflammation is more important than worrying about cholesterol.

America's health care industry doesn't acknowledge the wide ranging sources of health care that have been significantly helpful to me. Only one of the health care discoveries listed above is covered by my health insurance. None of these treatment protocols were prescribed by insurance-covered doctors. The American medicine "experts" have gone through rigorous classroom, laboratory, and intern training. Each one chooses the rigor and dedication level they put into keeping up with constantly evolving research. They even learn as they do the "talking shop" routine at social gatherings. All that training and the expense to get it didn't help me.

America's mainstream medical doctors come out of what I call Med School Mentality Medicine (MSMM) institutions. Med schools promote algorithmic actions—there's a set of correct diagnostic tools, and once something is diagnosed there is a prescribed what-to-do list. In my opinion and from my experience, America's dominant health care model is narrowly focused. What results from such focus is not unlike the outcome of the blinders that were put on farm horses so they wouldn't be distracted by what's going on elsewhere. I've experienced a frustrating lack of willingness by MSMM doctors to think out of the box in order to customize how they respond to individual patients. The MSMM book and insurance industry pretty much dictate how they think and act. Tunnel vision doesn't work for outliers like me.

Health care professionals have a difficult task when we ask them to fix us. Diagnosis starts by knowing what the symptoms are. Lab tests often are very telling, but patient reporting is also necessary. We are often not very articulate in expressing what we think we know, so doctors need to guess, often need to translate what we are saying into MSMM lingo. Health care must constantly evolve to respond to diseases more common elsewhere on our planet. Human bodies respond differently to different environmental health-affecting factors, such as the vast array and poorly studied use of chemicals. More and more people are intolerant or allergic to more and more things. Our needs, obvious or not, can be very diverse. Mental health. Obesity and lack of exercise. Drug abuse.

Providing effective health care *is not easy to do*! My

complaint is not with the health care professionals in any clinic or hospital I've gone to. These people seem very dedicated. It's the MSMM institutions that shaped them. It's the system, the business models. It's the strangle-hold influence of insurance and pharmaceutical company leaders and their lobbyists, and the backboneless members of Congress.

A growing number of Americans are becoming wiser about their health care, which is smart regardless of the medical system. Many are eating better, exercising more, reducing stress, sleeping more, etc. Many are checking out options for whom to consult and engage in diagnosing and treating health problems: chiropractic, acupuncture, naturopathic, and other options.

I've let off some steam in this chapter. I need to say that I've needed and will continue to need health care from MSMM professionals. I'm not throwing out the baby with the bathwater. It's just that America needs to look beyond the way-we've-done-it model to find, in many cases rediscover, health care options that fit our unique health care needs.

We're all unique and require inquiring health-care minds to determine just what we need to stay healthy or return to health. We need professionals who are very aware of the *total body*—all of its bones and glands and organs, all of its systems. Each amazing part of the body can function together as created when dedicated health professionals work with us to educate, diagnose, and treat.

Q_s

1. What has been your experience with health care provided by America's dominant health care providers?

2. If you've tried alternatives to Med School Mentality Medicine, what has been your experience? Positives? Negatives?

3. What are your thoughts about prescribed medicines?

4. If you could design what insurance company policies would look like, include and exclude, what would be the result?

Post Script: My hat is off to the many doctors of all types who have worked so hard to care for me. Among them are Dr. Glenn, Dr. Ralph, Dr. Sherlyn, Dr. Yongping, Dr. Jennifer, Dr. Jeffrey, and Dr. Craig.

Chapter 8

Gut Wrenching Politics

**America suffers when we lose the attitudes
and skills needed for civil discourse.**

I was heading back to my car on a 2015 summer day after
buying some house project stuff at our neighborhood hardware store when Pete and I spotted each other in the parking
lot. It'd been six years or so since we had last seen each other.
It felt good to reconnect even though ours was a distant cousin
relationship.

Pete asked me if I was still on Bloomington's City Council.
Smiling, I said I hadn't been recalled yet. (My body instinctively goes into alert mode when I hear references to my being
on a city council, so I typically try to start with something
light.) A couple more catching up comments between us and
Pete relaunched his trip to the store.

A few paces and he stopped. He turned around and asked,
"Did you hear that Richfield's Council pre-empted any efforts
by those who may want to sell marijuana in our city? Are you
going to do the same?"

I was confused a bit. The Minnesota Legislature had established a process to ease into selling medical marijuana when it

recently passed legislation permitting it. But it sounded to me that Pete was talking about social use.

I mentioned that I was aware of the basic start up provision of the statute—that one dispensary location was going to be authorized for each of Minnesota's Congressional districts. I added that Bloomington staff was researching the issues to help the Council decide if we should at some point consider providing a purchase location for those who had prescriptions.

Pete's response was prompt in pointing out his view. "Medical marijuana is in pill form, but it won't be long before it'll lead to sale of the smoking kind!" Comments about what was happening in Colorado spilled out in equally rapid fire fashion. I said "Pete, you're pretty worked up." He agreed. (I like people who know who they are and are open in acknowledging that.)

Perhaps it was an attempt to explain the possibility that Bloomington might end up with the first 3rd District dispensary but I heard myself saying, "There are some people who have a health issue that, medical doctors say, benefit from marijuana." Pete agreed but quickly moved on to describe disturbing stories coming out of Denver. I nodded acknowledgement that I'd heard such stories.

We parted a second time, seeming to agree that medical marijuana was okay, but social use was another story. A few more paces, however, and Pete turned and called out two more topics that obviously were also on his highly agitated mind. "It's Obama! We need to close down the borders! And Social Security—we've gotta catch people that are claiming it when they don't deserve it!"

He didn't wait for my response. He turned again and made

it all the way to the store this time. I was relieved that our "reunion" was over.

Opening the door to my car, I realized I was worked up too. The upbeat start to our seeing each other after so many years had quickly deteriorated, and I wasn't sure how that happened. I spent the ten-minute drive home trying to figure out why.

I recalled the stomach knots I often felt back in 2010. I remembered needing to turn off the radio or TV news. My anguish when hearing the bickering going on in my country during that presidential campaign year was why I made a furtive attempt to run for Congress as an independent.

Was the way Pete came across to me yet another flashback to the agony I felt five years earlier? I decided, yes, my reunion with Pete produced the same tension in the gut I'd experienced in 2010. Such feelings occur less frequently now because I've taken evasive action. The run for Congress helped, writing this book helps, and serving on my city's council helps. I feel a bit better because I'm taking concrete steps to try to change the angry atmosphere in my country.

Nonetheless, I have moments when a variety of emotions grab me as the partisan bickering has gotten even worse. "Everyone" talks about how bad it is at the Federal government level, but it happens in state and local governing too. We even experienced heated arguing, name calling, and physical hostility when the Bloomington City Council studied, and then voted to adopt, organized solid waste and recycling pickup.

Sadly the partisan bickering has infiltrated our culture. It's affecting faith communities, neighborhoods, even families. Such attitudes and behaviors are embedding themselves as a normal way of life instead of being seen as an operable wound being inflicted on our way of life. Strings of thoughts like this produce a feeling of dread in me.

I'm at a point in my life where I instinctively want to pull away from obviously partisan people (whether Democrats or Republicans), from vehement, impassioned, and often loud voices that earnestly make strongly-worded partisan statements. Voices in the middle can quickly get caught in the crossfire. Countering an emotionally stated partisan statement with questions and efforts to insert relevant information is viewed as a counterattack from an enemy, even when areas of agreement outnumber disagreement.

Once I heard how riled up Pete was, I pressured myself to disengage as quickly as possible in order to avoid getting into an argument. I'm not one to walk away from challenges. I thought my calm-voiced comments were a decent mix of agreement with him about medical marijuana and attempts to put some mainstream America thinking on the table. But it was clear to me that my efforts to do point/counterpoint weren't going anywhere.

A "what's the use" feeling returned in me, like it has too often when I have talked with a very partisan person.

A word surfaced as I continued my effort to understand what had happened: wild-eyed. My sense of where Pete was coming from was that his emotions had revved up to such a level that he wasn't interested in hearing anything that didn't fit with what he passionately believed. I didn't want Pete to think I accepted his style, but I knew from experience that the chances that we could get to a reasonable dialog were nil. Tension in the mind, tension in the gut.

I get frustrated when individuals on both sides of issues that divide our polarized nation close their minds to other ways of seeing the issue. I see wild-eyed people on the *far left* and the *far right*. Such strategies (or is it selfish blindness) do nothing to productively make America a good nation.

I decided my efforts to disengage and end our reunion as quickly as possible was rooted in a desire, a visceral need, to not participate in unproductive bickering. My instinctive attempt to promote calm, thoughtful dialog didn't work. My inborn desire to move Pete and me (and our nation) away from such heated rhetoric failed. Instead I simply felt mentally bullied.

Fact is I'm fed up with closed-minded thinking. I've seen how intimidated some people can become when addressed with strongly-worded, even threatening, outbursts. Sometimes the intimidators also speak loudly about the importance of defending democracy. Patriotic *words* about democracy do not alone make American democracy stronger; a healthy democracy requires civil dialog. Browbeating others into fearful submission with threatening words, tone of voice, and body language crush the very dialog upon which a democracy depends.

What is going on in America that such scenes have become so common? Somehow we have to find answers. America suffers when we lose the attitudes and skills needed for civil discourse in order to problem solve and strategize the future. We need to work together. Chance reunions in a hardware store parking lot shouldn't end the way my encounter with Pete did that day.

Note: This chapter was written in early summer 2015. I leave it to readers to update it for the 2016 national campaign season.

Q_s

1. Have you been confronted by someone who strongly states their view about an issue and you get the sense that anything you might state as a different view would lead to a bad argument? If so, how did you feel? What did you do?

2. Much is said and written about how polarized America has become. If you agree, how do you think we got this way?

3. What needs to happen to move the resolution of controversial issues into a more productive direction? What can and will you do? What will happen if we the people—all of us—don't get back to more civil give and take?

Chapter 9

Defensiveness

**Defensiveness permeates life; managing
how we cause it and how we respond to it
improves relationships.**

My wife and I decided to check out a home and garden show
on a Saturday one February. We didn't have any particular
needs, but sometimes it's good to escape the hectic activity that
seems to dominate our lives and do something relaxing.

Our pace was at the mosey speed, and we did really well
going with the flow, even when one of us wanted to talk to a
vendor about a personal interest that wasn't a mutual interest.
We were relaxed.

About halfway through the tour we were drawn to a vendor
who enticed us there by asking if we liked hot chocolate. A good
move, I thought, noting the chilly wind we had experienced
walking to St. Paul's River Centre from the parking ramp. He
poured a little milk or cream into a clear glass bowl and energet-
ically pumped the mechanical whisk he was selling.

The liquid quickly foamed up and I began to salivate. I
thought we were going to get a taste of some hot chocolate.
The man knew he wouldn't have our attention for long. He

shoved the bowl aside and immediately started talking about other uses for the whisk. He redirected my taste buds to scrambled eggs. The whisk was multi-talented! It would almost instantly fluff up eggs to give us the lightest omelets we could possibly imagine. The demo was pretty impressive.

A slight pause in his presentation gave me the opportunity to blurt out, "Do they sell for five bucks?" The vendor's response was instant and definitely mood changing. "You insult me!" The tone in his voice and the look on his face, in his eyes, told me I'd hit a touchy nerve.

Now I'm aware that humor can go awry. This wasn't the first time I'd personally found that out. These situations happen in a flash. I made an attempt to tell him I didn't mean to insult him. But I quickly realized trying to explain what I meant—that I expected him to come back as playfully as I had intended my comment—wasn't working. Sandy and I simply moved on.

We moved away quickly. Out of earshot of the man, we exchanged comments about what had happened. We agreed he didn't seem to be the kind of person usually seen in sales. We wondered if he would make many sales that day.

As we tried to retrieve the strolling feel that accompanied our strolling pace, I mulled over the incident. I wondered if something was going on in his life that led to his sharp response. I even wondered if I should feel bad about upsetting him if life wasn't going well.

But I also felt upset. Upset that he would verbally jump on me like he did. Wouldn't anyone else have realized I was kidding, simply wanting to get an idea what this device cost? I hadn't intended to upset him. Yet somehow I triggered a defense mechanism—big time.

It's a habit with me to try to understand other humans, as well as myself. Over the next few days my mind would occasionally wander back to the incident.

The defensive mechanism strikes me as being one of the most deep-seated, primal human reflexes we have in us. When we feel insulted, we instinctively feel a need to defend ourselves. Emotions flare and we lunge into a response of some sort. Depending on our personality we react with a counter-attack or maybe simply feel hurt.

I recalled seeing the defense mechanism in action many times during my thirty-three years as a teacher and principal. In the middle school setting I saw it lead to fights, bring on tears from hurt feelings, and lead to dueling verbal jabs. I saw it break up friendships, at least temporarily.

Working with young teens taught me a lot about human nature; they are in the raw so to speak, part child and part adult. They tend to be less inclined than the average adult to hold their tongues, less capable of hiding their feelings. My years as a junior and senior high school educator provided me with a pretty revealing laboratory. The adult lab world isn't much different, except that we adults tend to hide or mute our responses when we feel insulted or disrespected in some way. Defensiveness is a dynamic that permeates daily life for people of any age.

We are vulnerable to putdowns and criticism when, at our core, we don't feel we're worthy, likeable, or competent. When someone stabs us with words that bring our worthiness into question, we have that primal need to protect ourselves. So it is understandable that we'd push back, jab back. By putting someone else down we are trying to regain status—in our own minds or in the eyes of others. If we put down the person we perceive to be attacking us, we convince ourselves that we look comparatively better; we regain some of the image loss the other person's put down may have created in us. The tit-for-tat exchanges that often erupt are really two people each trying to feel better about themselves by degrading the other. Unfortunately that process produces a downward spiral in the relationship. The spiral takes on greater significance to the extent that other people are sucked into the situation.

We're better off when we achieve a basic understanding of the dynamics of defensiveness. That needs to include understanding what's going on when we get defensive, as well as when we realize we've caused someone else to become defensive. It's a primal phenomenon that the human species may never fully manage well. We can, however, manage it better.

I had never seen the whisk man before the three minutes of our interaction at the home and garden show. I'll never see him again. But I hope ruminating about that cold February day helps me think through and plan strategies that will help me fix situations when I create defensiveness in someone. I know I can't control how others might react to my comments, but I can work on becoming more aware. I'm working on the flip side too, trying to better chill the "strike back" instinct that lurks in me.

Q_s

1. How often in a typical day do you sense you've gotten defensive? Is it easier to see defensive reactions as an observer of other people than in yourself?

2. What payback do you get when you develop attitudes and learn skills that help someone else talk through and fix defensive reaction episodes?

3. "It's not what you say but how you say it" is a guideline many of us have picked up at some point in our lives. Have you found other wise sayings that help you decrease the likelihood that you'll do or say something that produces a defensive reaction in someone at work? In your neighborhood? In your family?

Chapter 10

Standard of Living

**Consider a new standard of living definition
that fits your "good life."**

I have never had to worry about having adequate food, clothing, and shelter. As a kid I never thought twice about playing a sport, joining Boy Scouts, or going to a camp. Parent finances even permitted purchase of an old cabin on a lake when I was eleven. Lake Belle Taine time meant fishing, swimming, water skiing, canoeing! I had a lucky start in life.

My lived-through-the-Great Depression parents gave me that start by pulling themselves through years of "living okay with little"—reusing things like store bread bags, re-covering worn furniture instead of buying new, generally not living "high off the hog," saving, and planning financially. Two major outcomes resulted from their efforts: my sister and I could go to college and they could retire comfortably.

It's partly because I learned to model what I saw my parents doing, that I'm doing well today. Being born in 1945 didn't hurt either. World War II ended a few months after I was born, and the job market stayed strong for years, due in part to an economic boom created by the war. I had no problem getting a job right out of college—life was good for me and most Americans.

> *Standard of living: 1. the necessities, comforts, and luxuries enjoyed or aspired to by an individual or group; 2. a minimum of necessities, comforts, or luxuries held essential to maintaining a person or group in customary or proper status or circumstances*
>
> *(Merriam-Webster Dictionary)*

Then and now are different. The effects of The Great Recession that started around 2007 are still messing with the quality of life—the standard of living—for too many Americans. While I'm doing well, I feel for those still struggling to recover. They may never do so. Is this the legacy America leaves for most of its children?

I wonder how economically well-off my grandchildren will be as adults. I wish I could tell them that America finally learned from the lessons many recessions have taught us. I wish I could tell them we won't have more of them. But I know such lessons need to be re-learned again and again, in part because the world changes, human nature does not, and that mix guarantees we'll have economic ups and downs.

There are some ways I can help prepare my grandchildren for such eventualities. I can mention that it's good to save for a rainy day. I can tell them that I'll be happy for them and with them when their finances—from piggy bank days to buying their first car—make them feel good. I hope I won't need to commiserate with them when their finances go south. I expect I'll get the chance to talk with them once in a while about how the past doesn't always predict the future, that there are no guarantees that their lives will be economically comfortable.

America's children and grandchildren can't expect that their incomes will always provide them a good standard of living. Recessions happen. Bad injuries and debilitating health changes happen. Hurricanes and tornados happen. Human-caused calamity, like war on our soil, can happen.

For many of us, simply living in America greatly improves our chance of enjoying a high standard of living. The living-in-America advantage is changing though. Global economics dynamics are less responsive to American "wishes and commands." Global realities are clearly signaling that the preeminence that America has enjoyed on Planet Earth is no longer a given. The past doesn't always predict the future.

The human reality that the future is ultimately not predictable means we need to plan for that phenomenon.

America is known for its striving people. There's a standard-of-living-is-important feel in our nation. We somehow became a culture that emphasizes the importance of comparing ourselves to others on how well we're doing economically. As a child I heard adults mention "keeping up with the Joneses." It wasn't long ago that a TV commercial for an automaker reminded me of the keeping-up pressure in our culture. A man was shown complementing his neighbor on a new vehicle, and then, like he set up the neighbor, he pushed a remote to do something on his "mine's-better" new vehicle in his driveway.

We have it in us to plan for the "what ifs" of life. As part of that planning we need to think out of the box. I think it's time to rethink and at least add another dictionary definition of *standard of living*. Let's rethink what standard of living *should mean* instead of staying with what it *has meant.*

We obviously need to be motivated to work, earn an income to support ourselves. Going beyond food, clothing, and shelter is okay to a point. But I think we've been seduced by the match-or-exceed-thy-neighbor's-wealth cultural forces. We're looking at the standard of living concept in the wrong way. We need to rethink what a truly happy human really needs.

Many Americans, influenced by forces in our culture, are engaged in a pervasive, sometimes mentally and physically frantic quest to raise their standard of living by doing all they can to make more money. Could such stress contribute to America's high medical costs, including mental health care?

We need to take a deep breath, take a self-searching look into what's most important to us, and reflect about what we see. What values do we really cherish? Which families and communities do we admire because they demonstrate attributes that we know, down deep, represent living the good life without lots of moolah? What legacy do we want to leave our children and grandchildren?

We don't need to join a convent or live alone deep in the woods. That life may define the good life for some. What we all need to do is the soul searching that helps us define the good life specifically for us.

I believe we've become confused, that we think standard of living is how much stuff and money we have. No wonder! That's how we've generally viewed standard of living. We need to wonder if we've gotten sucked in by societal norms, snookered into thinking that a financial standard (the amount of purchasing power we have) is what it's all about. Isn't it really more the non-stuff stuff, the hard to measure aspects of life that human beings really need to seek?

Q_s

1. We see daily updates on how well Wall Street economic indicators are doing. Does this information tell us how well individual Americans are living?

2. How do you describe "good quality of life"? What does it take to achieve this quality of life? What requires money, what doesn't?

3. Have you had experiences that caused you to, at least for a while, count your blessings in ways that go beyond what more money could buy?

4. At what point does a very low income mean a person cannot have a reasonably good quality of life? Do some Americans ignore people in poverty by saying "you don't need much money to have good quality of life"?

5. There's a Christian statement, a tenet also promoted by other world religions, that goes something like: What does it profit a person if they gain things of this world and never seek and incorporate into their lives what's really important. To what extent do you think you've discovered what's really important? What are the standards you use to determine how well-off you are?

Chapter 11

The Rest of the Story

What influences shape the evolving life stories of our kids?

I got the chance to be outside, make some decent money, and add another experience to my budding resume when I worked for the U.S. Geological Survey the summer of 1967. The change of pace from previous summer jobs provided a nice transition from Halstad High School graduation to my freshman year at Concordia College. Also, the job introduced me to the idea that there's always going to be "the rest of the story" no matter how much we already know about a person.

We were a summer team of two, the experienced professional who knew what he was doing and an eighteen-year-old eager to be outdoors and willing to learn—and walk a lot. My boss's assignment was to draw topographical lines on a map. My job was to carry a hinged 1" x 4" board with markings calibrated in feet and inches.

Each day we'd start from a benchmark with very precise elevation and location information that had been established years earlier by other crews beaming light rays on clear nights. I'd rest the bottom of my board on that marker and flip it up to its full fourteen-foot height so my boss could read it through his transit scope. We leapfrogged across the countryside so he could track and sketch in contour lines at five-foot intervals.

Interesting work I lucked into. I learned a lot about surveying. I also enjoyed our lunch breaks. My boss was intent on planning lunch breaks so we could catch Paul Harvey's noon-hour program on the truck's radio. Harvey died years ago, but many of us can recall his distinctive voice and commentary style as though we were listening to him right now. His voice was clear. His speech patterns emphatically changed pitch and volume. He used pauses so effectively that you'd stop crunching on an apple to make sure you didn't miss what he was going to say next.

Story telling was one of Harvey's signature means of grabbing listener attention as he editorialized about American life. He'd start a story but then break for a commercial, promising to come back with "the rest of the story."

That phrase came to mind as I was driving home from our church's retreat for kids at a Northern Minnesota camp on a fall weekend. That setting, with cell phones and other electronic devices banned, meant forty hours of focused time with middle school kids and an opportunity to observe and get to know them.

I wondered if their life stories were similar to mine when I was moving into my teenage years. I wondered how they were responding, how they were being shaped by the changes that have happened since I was their age. About a third of those on the retreat had recently entered teen years, the period of time when humans take on more and more responsibility for their future. Paul Harvey's "the rest of the story" way of describing the news slipped into my drive-time musings.

Major decisions were seeping into the minds of the kids I got to know a little during our two night retreat. They were starting to grapple with how to make a living, how to move relationships with the opposite sex beyond the goofy stage, whether or not to get married, where they'd live, and whether or not to follow in their parents faith-life mold.

We adults had been invited to come along, invited to contribute to conversations about issues that our decades of post-teen experiences discovered were very important. I'd been impressed with how open and thoughtful many of these legally-under-aged kids were. Good kids with good noggins and adult support systems, and yet I wondered, even fretted a bit about, what "the rest of their stories" would be.

Middle school kids get information from a host of sources—families, friends, tweeting who knows who; and for some, news casts, print media, blogs, and such. Each source influences how their lives, how their stories unfold. What will the impact of such a broad base of influence be? Will the positive influences outweigh the negatives?

I also wondered what impact the human reality of gossip would have on how the rest of these kids' stories would unfold. People talk about each other, and such talk affects our stories as they evolve. I overheard a huge amount of such talk in the middle schools where I worked. The comments ranged from snide to complimentary. Such talk makes its way throughout schools but also continues in all kinds of settings throughout our lives.

Whether or not the content of gossip—positive or character assassinating—becomes known to a person, it will affect how the person develops. It affects how other people think of you. It may affect who likes or dislikes you. It may have an effect on who goes out of their way to help you get through life. There are dynamics that affect our life stories that we may never know about.

Paul Harvey was right. There's always more to a story. He knew what the rest of his broadcast story was before the network went to commercial time. Listeners like me had to wait to find out how the people in his story made out. That waiting piece is our reality. None of us, no matter what our age, knows how the rest of our stories will read.

I knew I had to be content with waiting to find out how the lives of the retreat kids turn out. At my age I won't know the ending of their stories, but I hope to keep track enough to get an idea of what direction their stories will ultimately take.

That's okay because that's the way it is. And knowing that simply means I'll be extra vigilant in looking for opportunities to do the little things that may help kids experience happiness and true success as the rest of their stories unfold.

*Q*s

1. You probably interact with young persons in your extended family, neighborhood, faith community, or elsewhere. How do you determine what role you can play in helping them shape the rest of their story? (Figuring out what's truly helpful can be tricky!)

2. What do you want the summary of your life story to be? What legacy do you expect to leave for your relatives? Your community? America?

3. Gossip spreads information that is typically incomplete and may be false. How can you manage negative gossip about you, correct it, and give a more complete story of who you are? What role should you play in reducing negative gossip about you? About others?

Chapter 12

Art and Darlene

**Core values support building and maintaining
good relationships and communities.**

My wife and I joined a new workout place close to our home
in early 2015. Seeking "replacement friends" for those we'd had
at the more distant Y required venturing out with small talk.
"I see you're wearing a T-shirt from Arizona," resulted in a
discovery that a stranger and I shared a connection to Tucson,
where I went to grad school, and to Sun City, where my broth-
er-in-law and his wife recently bought a place.

Another attempt to find workout friends occurred one Saturday morning with Darlene and Art. It looked to me like they
were perplexed, perhaps as first-day users. The fitness center's
grand opening occurred just weeks earlier, so I asked them if
they were just starting their membership. Their "yes" answer
moved quickly to their description of a dilemma they were in.

Turns out they'd put car keys and billfolds in one of the
available small safes, needed to retrieve something, and discovered rotating the dials the way they understood the directions wasn't working. I related to that, recalling anxiety that I
feel when locking such vaults in hotel rooms.

Even though neither of them could get their stuff, they didn't sound agitated. Voices were calm. Neither blamed the other. We knew that staff that could open the safes at this 24-hour business didn't arrive until noon, over two hours later. Darlene got on her phone to see if a relative would be able to pick them up. Problem solving attempted, but no solution resulted from that call. As Darlene got ready to try a second phone number, Sandy and I offered to drive them home. We were almost done with our workout, so it was no big deal.

Unsuccessful with the second call, they accepted the ride offer. A little more calm conversation between them and it was decided Darlene would stay to start her workout and we'd bring Art to their apartment a mile or so away to get a spare car key. One piece of luck in their bad-start day was that their carless son was there to let Dad in.

Though a quiet guy, Art engaged with us in conversation, further evidence that the couple was pretty easygoing. We found out they'd lived in the apartment seven years, moving there from a home they had owned in a suburb just north of Bloomington. Art matter-of-factly stated they needed to sell in order to have money to help out a son.

Sandy pulled into a parking spot, and Art walked in to get the keys. Our wait time gave us a chance to see that their apartment complex was maintained well. Surrounded by single family homes mostly built in the '60s and '70s, it looked to be well managed. Located in my city council district, I had heard earlier that it was a popular housing choice for Minnesota Viking players in its hay day. Musings ended as Art reappeared from his apartment building.

Perhaps it was the waiting time that promoted reflection.

Sometimes having down time is all it takes. Whatever the prompt, Sandy and I had an opportunity to realize the significance of our twenty to thirty minutes with two individuals who were total strangers before this chance encounter brought us together.

We had just interacted with two human beings that tend to blend into the surroundings—people who go about life without stirring up a fuss; people who take care of their needs without expecting much from anyone else. We'd been gifted with a little peek into the lives of this fifty-something couple, people who really are the bedrock of American society.

A simple thought spilled out in my words to Sandy after we brought Art back to the fitness center and doubled back to our home. "You know, we really undervalue people like Darlene and Art in our society, don't we?"

For some reason this brief encounter with Art and Darlene removed a veil covering my eyes. I actually saw two strangers that Saturday morning. Two individuals, much more like me than not. But also special. Special in the very fact that they took care of family, assuming that problems they had were theirs to solve. Special in that they realized freaking out about being locked out of their keys and billfolds was best handled by calm discussion. Special in leaning on a married relationship they'd shaped over the years to manage situations like the pickle they were in.

America loses out when we let ourselves ignore the value of the gifts that the "steady Eddys and Bettys" of our nation give to our communities. Darlene and Art modeled important values and behaviors that too many of us need help with: Calm problem solving, personal skills to work out personal problems, and the art of building and maintaining good relationships with spouses, children, neighbors and friends. These are the very people who become perfect safety nets for us when we need a little help, because they are familiar, trustable, and close at hand.

We are wise to include some Darlenes and Arts in our friendship circle.

*Q*s

1. How can we as individuals acknowledge, honor, and demonstrate appreciation for the Darlenes and Arts of America?

2. How do we train ourselves to notice them and engage in a way that promotes our learning from them?

3. One take-away from this chapter could be that humans fall into two groups: those that somehow demand attention and those who go about their business, their daily lives, without asking for the attention of others. In what ways does America need both?

Chapter 13

Yankee Ingenuity

**Growth and success springs from curious,
problem-solving, inventive minds.**

It's great that we have a lot of inventive, practical minds in our country. I saw an example one day at The Y. Some remodeling work was being done along a wall in the large exercise and strength building room. A segment of the wall was enclosed by a lightweight plastic sheet that went from floor to ceiling, at least twenty feet high. I presumed that one of the reasons it was there was to contain dust created by the workers.

What struck me was how the plastic was held in place. The workers who put it there didn't need a tall ladder to secure the plastic to the very high ceiling. The time needed to position the dust barrier was short. They didn't use duct tape or another product that might leave a sticky residue.

No, they used something really ingenious—effective, simple, and very efficient. Imagine a telescoping pole like those used to hold up tents, the type that you twist to lock in at the length you want. About eight of these long poles were equipped with a small Velcro® pad at the top. The edge of the plastic sheet had the other part of the Velcro. All the workers had to do was attach the Velcro on the plastic with the pole's Velcro, telescope up the poles with plastic and snug the plastic up against the ceiling where they wanted it. Presto, they were ready to start the dirty work!

> *"Yankee ingenuity is a stereotype of inventive-*
> *ness, technical solutions to practical problems,*
> *'know-how,' self-reliance and individual enterprise*
> *associated with the Yankees of New England and*
> *developed much of the industrial revolution in the*
> *United States." The phrase reportedly was coined as*
> *the Erie Canal was being built in the early 1800s.*
>
> (Wikipedia)

What I saw reminded me of stories I've heard in my lifetime that referred to *Yankee ingenuity*. My Uncle Irv was a great improviser even though he was born and raised in Minnesota and not a *Yankee*. Yankees certainly have no corner on the ingenuity market! My young mind was awed by all the creative things he could do. Uncle Irv claimed he could fix almost anything with baling wire. His smile told me he was stretching the truth some, but a look around his hobby farm revealed the creative ways he fixed and made things with "unique methods," often at little or no cost. I think his creativity grew out of necessity given that he grew up during the economic stresses of the Great Depression.

Uncle Irv's inventiveness, his ability to come up with technical solutions to practical problems, helped support his family during a time when resources were hard to come by. I'm sure he got a kick out of how wide-eyed I was about what he could do.

For the colonists and depression-era Americans like my Uncle Irv, Yankee ingenuity was a necessity for surviving during tough times. But some people simply are inventive because of who they are. Some minds are especially curious, observant, and creative problem solvers. They think out of the box and get excited when they come up with something that's unique, helpful to themselves or to others.

Such people probably were gifted with some basic DNA help, but not born with an ability to think up a Velcro-plastic-pole invention. I wonder what happens during the development of these people that makes them so creative. A good education is important, though it doesn't all happen inside schools. In fact many inventors didn't do well in a formal schooling environment. It's likely that creative persons "get that way" through diverse pathways.

Any mind needs to develop so it can learn. A variety of factors matter, from the womb into early childhood—good nutrition, mental stimulation, and behavior boundaries that teach self-discipline without smothering a willingness to follow imagination impulses. A tough order for a nation to accomplish.

Sounds like parenting matters. It does, but there's more. Anyone in a young person's life matters. We all help shape another's mind when we compliment them for coming up with a creative solution to any problem on their own.

My experience with public school students and my own grandchildren suggests some of the best learning happens in short spurts, often started by a context-driven question or a simple compliment. We train the minds of others to be curious and analytic when we ask them how something happens. I remember watching in my elementary school classroom how food dye travels up a celery stalk that's placed in a glass with a dye-water mixture. I know that that experience influenced me to be more generally curious throughout my life.

In the workplace, employers foster creativity by rewarding people who offer good self-generated ideas with raises and promotions. Media and books report innovative ideas that may start in a garage or basement but turn into very successful businesses. Such public attention juices people to pursue an idle thought that they may have never pursued without seeing others get such adulation.

Yankee ingenuity is a great skill, a great attitude, a great value. It plays an important role for individuals but has also been a great boon to our nation by generating inventions and new businesses, improving safety, and creating cheaper or otherwise better products or services. People do figure out a better mouse trap by going beyond the idea of how to stop mice from doing stuff in our houses. In fact we now have to scan the shelves in the mouse product aisles of a hardware store to find one of those wood/spring contraptions that dominated the market years ago. Creative minds figure out alternatives to all sorts of thinking.

It certainly is not just those Nineteenth Century Yankees in New England that produced ingenious thought. The Chinese invented porcelain; the Egyptians came up with a math system; the Anishinabe (Ojibway) in north central United States made canoes from birch bark; and Europeans developed the printing press. Today, as in the past, America has done a good job of producing and supporting the entrepreneurial spirit.

Individuals who tap into their curious, problem-solving,

inventive minds do themselves a favor—and contribute to a better legacy for our kids. We will continue the growth and success of our nation to the extent we personally figure out how we develop, encourage, and support individuals with curious, problem-solving, inventive minds.

I wish I could track down whoever came up with the telescoping pole-Velcro-plastic idea I saw at the Y. I'd tell 'em "Way to go!"

Q_s

1. How do you feel when you come up with a creative idea for fixing something or figuring out a better way to do something? What impact does receiving a genuine compliment for your idea have on you?

2. Have you invested time, knowledge, and/or finances to help a kid in your neighborhood start a business, even one as small as a lemonade stand?

3. Do you know anyone who is an "angel investor" on either a large or small scale? What role do such investors have in shaping a healthy national economy?

Chapter 14

Community and Individuals

**How do we balance our needs with the needs of
communities and our nation?**

I moved into a neighborhood near the U of MN-Duluth campus in the early 1990s. The house was well built, in a convenient location, and homes in the area looked well kept. Turned out that the neighbors were the typical mix of outgoing and keep-to-ourselves types—all nice people.

One of the more gregarious neighbors and I talked fairly often, usually briefly in friendly exchanges across our narrow, quiet street. However, one of our longer talks in my yard toward the end of our first summer had a different feel. It put, for me, a slightly strained cast on our relationship. My neighbor brought up lawn mowing, noting that most people on our block mowed either Friday or Saturday. He commented about how nice the results looked.

I'm sure my facial expression and the sound of my voice contradicted my words somewhat. I tried to keep our good relationship intact by agreeing with his "nice look" comment. But I know that I instinctively was troubled by the clear inference that I should adjust my mowing habits to fit the norm he described. I like to mow my lawn when it needs it, based on height, and I believe it's best for the grass to be long enough to better shade the roots in hot weather.

I was conflicted. Something in me said it wouldn't be a really big deal if I tried to mow on Friday or Saturday, but I also felt I had the right to mow when and how I wanted. Unable to let the conversation simply slide, I stewed some. At one point I recalled some of the discussions I'd had with my students at Ordean Junior High. One of the courses regularly on my teaching schedule was Civics, and it was this course that came to mind.

One important goal for civics classes was to understand what the framers of The Constitution of the United States wanted our government to look like, how it should be structured. That meant I needed to help ninth graders in Duluth, MN, dig into the Constitution, studying each of its seven articles and the amendments that were made to modify or change it.

More complicated and more difficult to get our heads around was the *why* piece: why was our government designed the way we have it—what was the philosophy, the intended outcomes that the Founding Fathers (and Founding Mothers, mainly in the background) wanted to achieve. The *whys* revved up greater student interest than did the *whats*. I appreciated the energized dialog that occurred as we worked to understand the Preamble and its inspired, concise language.

The Preamble is essentially an introduction to our Constitution. It is a short (52 words) statement that in essence explains why such American legends as Washington, Jefferson, Franklin, Madison, and Hamilton literally risked their lives during the American Revolution. The Preamble explains what motivated them to put in many hours of often heated debate at the convention in Philadelphia where they met to hammer out the concepts and wording of our Constitution.

> *We the People of the United States, in Order to form a more perfect Union, establish Justice, insure domestic Tranquility, provide for the common defense, promote the general Welfare, and secure the Blessings of Liberty to ourselves and our Posterity, do ordain and establish this Constitution for the United States of America.*
>
> (*Preamble to the Constitution of the United States of America. National Archives and Records Administration*)

The young teens in my classes readily understood "more perfect union, justice, domestic tranquility" (with word definition help) and "defense" clauses in the Preamble. But "promote the general welfare and secure the blessings of liberty to ourselves and our posterity" was a different story. What does "general welfare" mean and how do you promote that? What are the "blessings of liberty"? And who should get them? The nation? Each one of us? Both nation and individual? Defining posterity was the easy part!

"Blessings of liberty." Students generally agreed that we didn't want anyone taking over our nation—a real concern as the former colonists realized how difficult it was to start a new nation, especially with lofty ideals. Students also didn't want to live in a country where people are dictated to instead of being permitted to participate in government.

But they also wanted freedoms for themselves as individuals. Believe me, I learned early in my teaching career how prone adolescents are to claim rights. And they're good at stepping up to support other students in the adults-in-charge structure of schools. The result is that most students sided with historians and other scholars who believe the Founding Fathers wanted to preserve liberty for the nation *and* individual Americans.

"General welfare." Groups of thirty-some adolescents in a classroom five times a week take on a community feel, complete with smooth and rough times. Factoring in adolescent hormonal changes, varied personalities, and mood swings, our opportunities to talk about what makes communities work or fail were significant and plentiful. We had opportunities to discuss real-time, real-life situations of how individuals wanted rights and why some individual rights needed to be modified because it made sense and helped us live together.

In a democracy, a nation governed by rule of the people, achieving this balance between personal freedom and what's good for our communities—of all sizes and types—is critical. It's a perennial challenge we must not ignore. It calls for a never-ending debate and effort that puts flesh on the concept of democracy, keeps it alive.

The never ending task before us is to figure out how collective, community rights legitimately need to modify our personal rights. Fortunately, there are some realities and natural motivations that help individuals, instinctively self-centered, *want* to make communities work well.

It was during my high school years when I got my first strong feeling of the importance of *community*. During that time my classmates and I worked together on school projects, performed together in music and drama events, played sports together, got into and out of trouble together, and together endured or enjoyed classes. We went to the drug store for cherry Cokes and to the restaurant after school events. Many of us did church stuff together. We roamed the streets just like in the movie *Grease* and television shows like *Happy Days*. We literally *felt* the value of community.

Social benefits are huge but there is more. When I worked with other students to produce the school yearbook in 1967, I found out how much better the result was because classmates had skills I didn't have, and it didn't take so long with a team effort. Playing my tuba in our band without other instruments would have meant I had constant pressure to be perfect, and the solo sound would not have had the richness and the harmony that forty-some instruments provided.

There are benefits to being part of a community, and there are challenges. Did I get into arguments with team mates during basketball practices? Yes. Did I resent others getting drawn up in plays that meant they would be shooting the basketball more than me? Yes. Were some of my ideas for the yearbook dropped in favor of someone else's? Yes. Did some guy take my favorite seat at the drug store and get more time talking to the girl I liked? Yes. In all these situations I wanted ME to be the center of the universe, to be the shooting star in basketball, to have my ideas chosen, to have the girl I wanted to be my girlfriend all to myself.

The trick for us as individuals is to exert self-discipline so that we advocate for ourselves while also advocating for a successful community. It's a matter of finding a good balance. It *does* come down to promoting the general welfare *and* securing the blessings of liberty for ourselves.

Hard work. Work that needs to be ongoing. The work to fulfill the noble goals that our Founders stated in our Constitution's Preamble is definitely worth that effort. I'd love to see how well the students in my 1970s-era civics classes are doing in making the balancing act work for them, and our nation.

How do I mow my lawn now? That neighbor's effort to promote yard harmony got me thinking. My grass is a bit taller than it is in the yards of some of my neighbors, but I learned it was okay for me to mow about the same day as most of my neighbors did. I smile now as I think about that uncomfortable conversation in the '90s. Balancing individual and community rights is possible. Perhaps America's Founders would smile about how this episode worked out—and join us in liking how the neighborhood lawns looked.

Q*s*

1. What internal conflicts do you experience when you try to balance your personal urges to have your rights along with the selfless urges to support the rights of your neighbors?

2. A thorny issue arose in Minnesota because of relentlessly cold temperatures one character-building winter. Some homes are heated with LP (liquid propane) gas. Getting tanks refilled became a problem as demand strained the availability of supply. The problem occurred also for another group of people. A second major consumer of this energy source is the farmer who uses LP gas to dry

crops that are too moist to store. Here are two groups of individuals with legitimately competing needs. Should one have a right to priority treatment? How should problems like this one be resolved?

3. The Founding Fathers talked about "civic virtue," the concept of living in such a way that our actions contribute to a successful nation. How well do Americans today live a life guided by civic virtues?

4. How do we remind individuals to think about the value of doing what's good for the neighborhood, the nation?

Chapter 15

We Live a Faith Life

Depending on others every day for many different reasons often takes a leap of faith.

One summer day about 4:00 pm, I was driving north on a 35 mph, four-lane county roadway that runs through Bloomington when I watched a car accident unfold. I observed helplessly as it became obvious two cars would crash in split seconds.

The eastbound car was not slowing down as it approached a stop sign. It sped past the sign, got hit by the car coming my way, spun around and plowed into a residence's cyclone fence. I pulled over and punched in 911.

I got out and talked on my cell phone as I hurried to the nearest crashed car. The eastbound driver was dazed but apparently not seriously hurt. The other driver had already gotten out of her car. I was relieved that those split seconds simply led to lots of problems but no serious injuries.

The accident shouldn't have happened. The driver who blew through the stop sign simply wasn't paying attention. That driver betrayed a trust by not adhering to traffic signs, by not following safe-driving thinking and behavior, not paying attention. The driver who was following the rules was victimized.

She lost some faith in other people that day.

We expect that a lot of things will go a certain way. Every day. We expect that a friend will keep a confidence. We expect that the anesthesiologist and surgeon will be competent and alert when "we're under." We expect people to follow directions on road signs, stay in their lanes, and a host of other safe-driving norms.

We typically assume that people will act as we expect them to act, even though we know there is no guarantee that they will. People let us down sometimes. We're all human, we make mistakes. Sometimes we act out of character, use poor judgment, or perform less competently than we usually do. Sometimes we're simply bad and intentionally defy societal norms and act out bad values.

Scholars—from philosophers to neuroscientists to poets to psychologists to theologians—tell us that humans have an inborn need to trust. It's important for us to go about our daily lives. We literally need some level of assurance that we can be safe in our vehicles, experience safe and successful surgery, have faith that a friend will treat us as a true friend would.

There is a rational element to trusting other individuals. It makes sense that personal experiences, repeated over time, will continue to repeat. It makes sense to believe that a close friend won't betray us because they never have over many years. The fact that we repeatedly drive to work, to an appointment, to the grocery store without getting into an accident supports a belief that we'll get where we want to go and back home just fine. Humans need such a rational sense of safety and security. Without it we would live in paralyzing fear. Trusting others is critically important for human mental health.

But the nature of trust in other individuals involves a counter-balancing dynamic: caution. There is no absolute guarantee that trusting another person will bring the results that faith expects. Being involved in a car accident teaches us that faith in others, even trusting yourself, requires a level of caution. When a friend breaks a long track record of keeping something confidential, it's natural to think twice before trusting the person again, and perhaps you might even be less willing to trust *anyone*.

Trust operates differently in personal friendships than it does when we interact with people we don't know. Ongoing close relationships mean we interact often with the others, know them well, and have a common history that would have ended if we didn't trust each other.

Chance interactions are a very different story. There is no basis to know whether we should or shouldn't trust a stranger. We don't have any reason to know the hundreds of drivers we may briefly glance at as we pass on a street or highway. We buy online from people we don't know.

Impersonal interactions are more an encounter than a relationship. What about trust in our daily impersonal encounters? Does the gas station operator give us a true gallon? What about doctors, first time in a barber's chair, lawyers, accountants, hotel housekeepers, financial advisors, and other service providers? Trusting people we don't know or barely know means we must believe, must *hope* that they are trustworthy to do for us what they say they will in a competent and ethical way.

Some trust-needing encounters aren't even face-to-face. Labels on stuff like breakfast cereal, new cars, prescription drugs, pesticides, and countless other products—are they accurate, true, and trustworthy? I've never met or talked to anyone who wrote any such label. Talk about blind trust!

Unfortunately, some people are periodically or regularly not trustworthy. Grandma introduced me to "bad apples" as a polite way to describe such individuals. Nobody likes to get burned by bad apples, be taken advantage of, bilked. Most people have a sixth sense and instinctively realize when someone isn't trustworthy. But some people are more vulnerable than others and become easy prey to the scumbags (sorry, Grandma) who take advantage of their inability to detect reasons to distrust.

Bad apples present a problem for society to resolve. What should be done when people get burned, taken advantage of, bilked? What can we do to prevent (realistically reduce) betrayals of trust that can/do occur? Does society have a responsibility to take steps to make sure labels are accurate and services are competent and provided through good faith, ethical efforts?

Does *society* in this context mean individuals and charitable organizations? Does *society* mean government? Should a combination of 1) individuals, 2) charity organizations, and 3) government be responsible for preventing and stopping the actions of America's bad apples when they erode the feeling of trust that we as individuals and we as a nation so basically need?

Producing answers gets complicated. Access to information is an issue. Authority to act is another problem. What rights do those accused of bilking someone have—for example, falsifying baby formula or stealing a pain killer prescribed for a homecare individual instead of giving it to the person at the appropriate time and amount? How would an individual or non-profit effectively handle such issues? Most ways to prevent or stop or punish bad apples require resources of time, money, and skills. Who should pick up the tab?

Words like trust and faith would not be in our vocabulary if life were totally predictable. We daily depend on other people to contribute to our wellbeing. We affect each other by how we live. We depend on others to drive safely; we depend on the teams who perform surgeries; we depend on others every day for a host of reasons. In all of these situations, we take a leap of faith.

Our nation is better to the extent *each of us* lives a daily life that others can depend on. Being worthy of trust is another way to be a patriotic American.

Q*s*

1. How do you promote trustworthy behaviors in your family or friendships?

2. Who should take the lead in assuming responsibility for defining, promoting, monitoring, supporting and enforcing our nation's trust standards?

3. How does the community in which you live promote, and in some cases require, trustworthy behavior?

Chapter 16

Jumping to Conclusions

**Kids and cowbells can help adults
learn good life lessons.**

Every once in a while I realize I jump to a conclusion that I later regret. Sometimes such conclusions are simply careless, based on sloppy thinking. Almost always I discover they were based on a prejudgment of some sort. I'm learning to think more before I leap; I want to avoid the regret I feel after drawing a hasty conclusion.

One learning experience occurred while in church on an Easter Sunday. Our church youth director invited kids to come up for a children's sermon. These one adult and a bunch of kid's interactions are brief in words and time and often unpredictable. They give kids that are just starting to walk through elementary school age some important stage time and "sermons" in words and images that are more effective for them.

On this particular Sunday the youth director brought a large suitcase full of little cowbells. The direction to the kids was to ring the bells like crazy every time they heard the word *alleluia* during the rest of the joy-filled Easter worship service. Of course they were up for that!

The interactive children's sermon ended and the kids returned to their parents. Each with a cowbell. They "practiced" quite a few times on the way back to their parents. Enthusiastically.

The bass sitting next to me in the choir balcony said, "This is going to be a problem." I agreed. Decades earlier, I was taught to be quiet most of the time during "anything church." Over time I realized and accepted, even embraced the idea, that church stuff shouldn't be so somber. But cowbells during a worship service? That just seemed like a bad idea. It was like giving kazoos to little kids before the Minnesota Orchestra started a performance.

I didn't hear the text reading very completely. It wasn't because of the rare, muted cow bell sound. It was because I was fretting about happy-go-lucky kids having them before they learned how to be serious and not adventurous in church. Although it now sounds Scrooge-like, I have to admit I was annoyed. Shouldn't parents silence the bells? But then I wondered what would happen if just one child was having a bad day or simply not prone to take directions from a parent. What would happen if even just one kid threw a tantrum when told to silence the bell.

My brain diverted some from the sermon, but then I started to relax. A flash back to when I brought my own children to church helped. I started to feel a bit sheepish as I vaguely remembered how Jesus said he wanted children to come to him and explained something about how we needed to be more like children.

I regretted what I had thought just moments earlier. Somehow I got back into the spirit of Easter, glad my thinking was redirected. The exuberance of kids and bells in church was a good message to me. Easter is telling a very joyful story central to Christian beliefs. The Bible talks about making a joyful noise! The choir, strings, wind instruments, brass, organ, and percussion would soon be leading the congregation in singing Handel's Halleluiah chorus—loud, high energy music. We'd be pulling out all the stops, making the church reverberate with sound.

Joyful sounds. Like kids do so well.

Personal preferences and perspectives, sometimes embedded in powerful ideological thoughts, develop throughout our lives—and not just in a faith-life context. We're affected by a lot of influences, from how we were raised to all sorts of life experiences. We develop attitudes—about our workplace, about how children should be raised, how schools should be run, what our policy should be toward China, and about all kinds of other things. Over time we get cozy with what we like. It becomes too natural and too easy to jump to conclusions based on our established attitudes.

By living in communities as we do we ultimately know we, as individuals, can't have it all our way. We're all different in some way. We need to consciously open our minds to the ways others think and do things, and recognize that values differing from ours have merit. The youth director was giving the children an opportunity to express Easter in terms their young minds could grasp. It certainly seemed to work that day.

My thinking did a 180 degree turn during that worship service. That experience was a good lesson, one I need to relearn whenever I realize I've jumped to a conclusion. I was very glad that I moved beyond my initial conclusion that all those bells in the hands of children were a bad idea. I'm glad that I came to realize I had judged the youth director's bells idea from a narrow, biased perspective.

I was so worried that I would be distracted from what was going on that I almost missed the wonderful sermon the children and their cowbells placed in front of me.

Q_s

1. Little children are naturally curious. How is it that adults lose that openness to the world and lose sight of, for example, a child's place in worship?

2. Much has been written about how differently Baby Boomers, Generation X, and millennials think about some dynamics in the work place. Whether a generational difference or something else, what value have you discovered in a colleague's contribution that you didn't notice earlier?

3. It seems to be human nature to sometimes draw conclusions too quickly. What works for you to avoid the embarrassment that results from a premature conclusion that turns out to be very wrong?

Chapter 17

Parka Hoods

**Take the time and make the effort to know others
beyond what is first perceived.**

Living in what some locals in Northern Minnesota affection-
ately call the tundra region gives me numerous opportunities
to realize how great it is to own a winter parka. One particular
parka went beyond its warming function by helping me gain
an insight about people. It happened one early morning while
I was a teacher in Duluth.

A thirteen-year-old was wearing that parka one blustery,
cold winter day as she entered Ordean Junior High School. She
was a walker, one of the students who lived too close to be eli-
gible for bus transportation and, presumably, lived in a home
where getting a car ride to school was either not workable or
not offered.

I was on hall duty. Young adolescents appreciate a warm
welcome as they come to school, even though a few aren't par-
ticularly enthused about school. Some also value the fact that
adults are there, either to protect them from trouble or to help
them stay out of trouble. Providing such noble service (administration "encouragement" makes it less noble) explains why I
was in the hall by my classroom door that morning.

I studied the girl's face to see if I knew her. Her face was all I could see since Velcro® held the hood shut to keep out the cold air. I was struck by how much her face communicated. A quick thought noted how routinely we miss the gold mine of information that faces feely offer.

I liked just seeing her face.

The "parka girl" flipped back the hood. She ran her hands through her hair to fix the inevitable hood-induced mess. She exemplified middle level school kids who pretty universally know how important it is to look right.

The girl's parka hood thrust into its resting place, she walked into her school day. I recognized her but didn't know her name. She was a student I'd seen during my lunchtime cafeteria supervision duty. It unsettled me a bit that I needed more than her face to remember her.

"The face" and the thoughts it provoked stayed with me. My eye, my mind, had been drawn to the girl's face the way artists get us to focus on what they want us to see. My eye was drawn to just the face because it was in such sharp contrast to the blandness, the unremarkableness of the parka that otherwise enshrouded her. The girl had a beauty that showed in her face when the rest of her was out of focus.

We rarely peer inside others to really get to know who they are. The *face experience* pointed out to me how much we base our understanding of other people on superficial things. I think we focus on others too shallowly for two main reasons.

We work to hide ourselves. The image we have of ourselves, about how we think others see us, is quite fragile. So we try to fix it up. Even people who seem very sure of themselves, even to the point of being cocky, spend time doubting how good, how smart, how skilled, how good looking they are.

A second major reason we see others on such a superficial level is that we have been commercialized. Our culture somehow has gotten to the point that we are convinced that anyone can make themselves adorable, cool, and competent. Check out how much money is spent on cosmetics and haircuts/adornments/coloring/etc. Note how tenuous clothing styles are, how short-lived before we need to catch up with the new, in styles. Skin tucks, tanning booths, eye glasses (whether needed or not), elevating shoes—the list of ways our culture lures us into thinking "we can be better" is very long. We do all this work and purchase all this stuff to modify our core identity to impress, attract—to change how we come across to other people.

A perfect storm of commercial products and services are promoted to convince us we're not so good but could look good and feel better if we just buy what they sell. There are forces in our culture that prey upon the very human reality that we have some level of doubt about how well we come across to other people. The forces are so seductive that it's no wonder we don't think first to get to know the inside person, the core of who a person is. Too often, how we perceive each other stems from peripheral stuff, from misleading first impressions.

Fortunately, many people have overcome the pressure to see others in a superficial way. They do take the time and expend the effort to peer into those they want to know, to support them and to be enriched by them. Some relationships need to start and stay at a surface level—with store clerks, some work place colleagues, even some neighbors and relatives. But some relationships really benefit, really blossom, when we mutually move in the direction of truly getting to know each other.

Opening up to someone we trust happens incrementally and benefits from patient intuition. Focusing on the face can help. The face is a physical phenomenon that is a unique part of the body. It's a direct conduit into what we're thinking but not saying, an indication of how we're feeling but not verbally expressing, and a sign of what we're needing but not asking for.

Getting to know someone well is a two-way street. I realize that I need to let people look into my uncluttered, unmade-up, unadorned core—to open myself to others in a genuine way. Doing that isn't easy! I'd rather cover myself. I'd rather figure out what would make me more likeable, more acceptable, and cover up whatever traits and image pieces of me that I don't want people to see. But the neat thing is that, when we together move beyond the superficial, we discover we are truly in the same boat—each of us has something we don't fully like about ourselves. When two individuals help each other get to the comfort zone of being okay—happy about who they are— they are in a much better place when it comes to responding to the inevitable ups and downs of life's realities.

The parka girl experience helped me realize the value of getting to know people beyond the superficial, the obvious. I work harder now to take the time and make the effort to get to know others beyond what I first perceive. I've discovered this effort requires patience, thinking out of the box, listening better, and stemming impulses to pre-judge.

A wonderful reward makes the work worthwhile. Doing so typically results in a reciprocal response that in turn leads to a truly genuine friendship. Mentally putting a hooded parka on a person might just help us focus enough on a person's face to discover a friend.

Q*s*

1. Humans need to cloak their identity at times. For what reasons, at what times, and in what situations do people need to protect their inner identity through peripherals like clothing?

2. What guides you in determining how you best help friends reveal more about who they are without probing too deeply?

3. Can we help improve racial relations in America by taking the time, exerting the patience, to develop the skills to intentionally work at getting to know and understand people beyond potential distracters like skin color, ways of speaking, cultural clothing (like hoods), and such?

Chapter 18

1998 and 2016

**Political parties need to connect better
with more than the party faithful.**

The campaign for the governorship in Minnesota in 1998 taught a lesson to political party leadership. Unfortunately, party leaders either never learned the lesson or quickly forgot it. The lesson was freely taught by Minnesota voters. The lesson, taught elsewhere and often, is that elected officials need to be connected to ALL Americans, connected so interactively that democracy is actively practiced and not just a hollow cliché.

As the 1998 gubernatorial election approached, two well-known men went through the party process of buttering up to influential people in the party, making a string of "I'll do what you want" promises along the way. It's a political party tradition in America.

The November 1998 ballot listed Republican Nick Coleman and Democrat Skip Humphrey. There were others—it's not uncommon in America for a few "also-rans" to file to get on the ballot. But the odds that someone without Democratic or Republican party support can actually win are essentially nil, so the choice really was either Coleman or Humphrey. In

1998 an also-ran was about to provide an exception to the rule, shocking people across the state and beyond.

The little-known person who shocked us was born James Janos. In later years he used his professional wrestler name, Jesse Ventura. Ventura had governing experience as mayor of a Twin Cities suburb. As we got to know him, we discovered he followed political issues on a broader scale, promoting such ideas as changing to a unicameral (one house) legislature and reviving commuter rail transit. He had his head into political issues. It's just that most often he was swimming against mainstream party thinking.

Ventura's wrestler-imposing size and his deep, commanding voice helped him carry his message to Minnesotans across the state. My recollection of his $300,000 campaign, including increasing TV news coverage as election day approached, is that he was not afraid to forcefully point out what he saw as the folly of many aspects of how government was run. A Ventura campaign slogan summed up his campaign well: "Don't Vote for Politics as Usual."

Jesse, conveying a folksy image, resonated with people who were sick and tired of the platitudes that flowed from slick politicians and were upset with politics in general. Jesse spoke bluntly, sometimes brashly. Many people loved it.

I was not impressed with either of the big party candidates but figured Ventura had no chance to win. I was ready to wait till morning to find out the result of this and other contests. But early reports intrigued me and I stayed up to watch.

Jesse the Body Ventura won. I recall thinking as he walked into his first victory interview: I bet he's wondering "Now, what am I going to do"? The look on Jesse's face, his voice, and how he spoke on TV that night suggested he was very surprised that he'd won. Just like pretty much anyone.

Shocking news like an election upset usually results in efforts to understand what happened and how to plan the future. Whatever wisdom resulted from such Democrat and Republican analysis was either short-lived or faulty. Ever since, America's election campaigns have spiraled increasingly downward into partisan bickering—and haven't responded to what most Americans want from election year campaigns.

The 2016 presidential campaign also has a politician outsider, in this case, someone who invited himself in as a big party candidate. Donald Trump is essentially mimicking Ventura's "Don't Vote for Politics as Usual" strategy. He's tapped into citizen disgust with politicians. As of this writing, he has become the Republican Party's nominee with very mixed responses. There is little question that he is benefiting from the fact the big parties have not learned that many, many Americans are fed up with political party leaders listening only to party insiders. Hillary Clinton, the Democratic Party nominee, an insider for a long time, has met stiff competition from Bernie Sanders, an insider who is acting more like an outsider. Many voters are not pleased with either major party candidate. As you read this, you may know the outcome of the November election.

The fact that lessons given eighteen years earlier were not heeded by Republicans and Democrats is telling. There is clear evidence that pent up frustrations are exploding among people whose needs have been ignored. Pent up frustration means that anger has taken over and anger usually reduces thoughtfulness. Honest, civil debate of issues has taken a back seat to negativism, to character smears, to aggressive and sometimes assaultive language and actions. We're seeing outright mean-spiritedness at a rate and level that, sadly, exceeds the usual not-good norm in campaigns.

It's hard, given this context, to figure out what candidates really think, and how they would act should they be elected. It's hard to know who to believe. That is a very chilling feeling since a successful democracy requires well informed voters.

What needs to happen to make America the thriving democracy it has been, can be? There is no single answer that explains why people in 1998 elected a relatively unknown (except in wrestling circles) person to become governor of Minnesota. There is no single reason that explains how dysfunctional the 2016 presidential election cycle has become. We need to study and learn from the lessons that Americans across the spectrum have been giving to political parties for a long time. American voters need and deserve:

- Transparency. We need the true character, the actual values of candidates, revealed. We need civilly-delivered direct, honest talk.

- Dialed back campaign budgets. The cost of running campaigns has gotten absolutely, insanely too high. Money talks (AKA buys influence). The amount needed today automatically means the vast number of Americans, even those who would make excellent representatives of the people, can never seriously think about running for any office except in some local governments.

- A more open candidate selection process. Political parties have made a mockery of democracy. They effectively control who will be on the ballot except for the also-rans who perennially tend to get no more than 5 percent of the vote.

- Good information. Biased information is not good information. Political parties have the partisan researchers (now isn't that an oxymoron) that know how to make falsehoods appear factual. They have experienced, slick-information spin doctors.

- Ethically guided emotion. Humans are a mix of thinking/reasoning and emotion/feeling drives. We are both because we need both. We need candidates who use emotional appeals appropriately, not manipulatively.

We must demand that candidates honor the bulleted list that describes what American voters need. It may seem that asking for such things is unrealistic. That is extremely sad. The list goes to the heart of what makes democracies work! We simply must work to make government, make our representatives, see the importance of responding to the issues that are so upsetting to so many Americans. We must not lose an understanding of what makes a democracy succeed. Let's learn from and positively respond to the lessons that the 1998 and 2016 campaign seasons give us.

Q_s

1. What do you need from candidates for elective office to help you vote?

2. There were some attempts during the 2015 phase of the 2016 election year cycle to form new organizations that would challenge the two dominant parties by using a nationwide primary approach to choose and support candidates, in other words, bypassing political parties. Why would you support, or not support, such attempts?

3. What does it mean to you that a growing number of Americans do not affiliate with any political party?

4. It's important to keep campaigns in America in perspective. Have they significantly changed during your lifetime? What made some better than 2016? In what ways were some worse?

Chapter 19

Role of Representatives

**The job description of elected representatives
should be straightforward and ethical.**

The first few months on Bloomington's City Council were all
that was necessary for me to discover that I wasn't the kind
of elected official that many people had learned to expect. I
decided I needed to come up with an opening statement to use
when I met with residents and groups with a stake in our city's
operations and future planning.

Credo: principle, view, belief, stand, philosophy
(Merriam-Webster Dictionary)

My philosophy and belief is straightforward. As an elected
official I must 1) get and work with good information, 2) work
hard to understand all points of view, and 3) decide how to vote
when the vote is called for, in other words, when I have the most
complete and up-to-date inputs from numbers 1 and 2.

I try to remember to put this credo on the mental table of
individual constituents and interest groups within the first
few minutes of any meeting. The responses are far ranging.
Some simply accept my statement, occasionally adding an

appreciative comment. Some react, somewhere on a continuum of responses that range from "Jon, that's not the way it's done" to "that's heroic" (blurted out by a participant during a day long workshop on government ethics held in St. Paul).

The three parts of my promise to myself and to the people of Bloomington look simple, but they involve some struggles. As noted in several other chapters, *getting good information* requires a lot of effort. Sources of information too often offer facts and figures as proof when in fact they are faulty, taken out of context, or are irrelevant, smooth-talking gibberish. And of course some important information is not readily available and has to be sought through digging around and asking a lot of questions.

Understanding all points of view is a constant challenge for humans in all aspects of life. Intentionally seeking this understanding is an especially important process when representing constituents in a democracy. Truly understanding what a person thinks and believes is no simple undertaking. This book digs into the complexities of communication and the diverse influences that shape the way each one of us thinks. This book also acknowledges the reality that how we think about some issues changes during our lifetimes due to changed circumstances and new life experiences. In other words, understanding the points of view of my constituents is a moving, complex target.

The time to decide how to vote is when a vote is called for, not when people prematurely ask for it. Every issue requires that I very consciously work on numbers one and two right up to the point of actually voting. What are the results of my searching for relevant information and doing fact checks? What are well informed city residents saying they want and need? What is the right thing to do? Part three of my credo creates a dilemma for some people. On the one hand, they realize good governing doesn't happen when decisions are made before all inputs are in. But on the other hand, they want the assurance that I will commit to what they think should happen.

Have I said that being a city council member can produce an occasional headache?

Two human nature problems raise their ugly heads and confront me as an elected official. One is the inescapable reality that I am a unique individual who brings my own values and life experiences with me when elected to represent others. I also come to the job with my own gathered-along-life's-way sets of information. The fact is that my perspectives need to be submerged when they differ from what the majority of my constituents need. The self-centeredness reality is a hard one to shake.

The other problem is an outcome that often occurs when new, significant power is given to a person. I started in office thinking I was no different than before being sworn in. My attitude is the same now, but that assumption has been proven wrong in a variety of ways. Comments and looks suggest that I am far less the ordinary guy people perceived me to be before starting my first term as a council member. A total stranger leaving the grocery store as I entered one day said, "Hello sir," in a soft-spoken voice. Sir! The sense I got is that he'd seen my picture in the monthly city newsletter or watched council meetings and he thought I deserved extra respect. I hope I've earned the respect he gave me in that brief encounter.

There *is* power that comes with being an elected official. As one of seven councilmembers, I have one-seventh of the authority to accept or reject policies that set the tone and direction of the City of Bloomington. The feeling-the-power problem can mess up the head and warp the genuine, lofty desires that many who seek election want to achieve. A feeling of power often clouds good judgment. Every time we elected representatives cast a vote we need to ask ourselves if the decision we're about to make is for the good of the community or in some way for our own benefit.

Two plus years into my term, I'm very glad, very comfortable with the path I embarked on in January of 2014. Democracy in America was set up by the Founding Fathers as a republic—we elect individuals to represent us, make decisions for us. I accept, even welcome, the challenge of representing sometimes polar opposite viewpoints and needs. The people and interest groups who are used to getting results from whatever degree of lobbying they use sometimes don't understand that other perspectives need my consideration. I'm not always successful in improving understanding, but some of the people who come to me with emotional outbursts that express very strong issue positions generally are accepting, perhaps grudgingly, the counter-point information that I pass on from other constituents.

Balancing the rights of some individuals with the rights of a community of individuals, of whatever size, is a challenge that elected representatives must take on. Doing so requires ethical thinking and actions. I've drawn my line in the sand. It feels right.

Q_s

1. What's on your job description list for those who represent you?

2. In what ways do you appreciate, and in what ways are you disappointed in, how members of Congress do the job of governing?

3. Representation occurs in many settings. Do your expectations of those who represent you differ across such groups as a PTA, a military unit, a labor union, a group of businesses, a wildlife group, a faith community council, and different levels of government?

Chapter 20

Role of Citizens

**Citizens honor America's Founders
by thoughtfully engaging
in the governing process.**

The schedule assigned to me my first year as a public school teacher included a course simply named Government. It was a requirement for all Duluth ninth graders for a very good reason—all individuals living in a democracy need to understand how our nation's government operates, why it was set up the way it was, and how citizens can (need to) participate.

This chapter will not turn into a lesson on how national and local governments operate, but it's important to be right up front about the context in which the role of citizens exists. The Founding Fathers of America wanted "the people" to have a huge voice in how government happens. The experience of having life-affecting decisions made by a king who lived across the Atlantic Ocean, a person who was not in touch with the colonists, was a type of government the Founders definitely wanted to avoid.

Republic: a government in which supreme power resides in a body of citizens entitled to vote, and is exercised by elected officers and representatives responsible to them and governing according to law.

(Merriam-Webster Dictionary)

The Founders therefore decided to structure The United States of America as a republic—the people elect representatives to run the government. That makes democracy, the rule of the majority, a common sense possibility. Imagine what it would be like if decisions were made by survey voting of all of the millions of us!

So how can a lone citizen do her or his part, perform a role in a republic? That's a challenging question. The answer starts with content in the government classes Americans have taken one way or another, either formally or in such personal efforts as learning by following the news and going online.

All Americans need to have at least a basic understanding of our nation's constitution. (To read online or print a copy of the U.S. Constitution visit www.archives.gov.) We need to know how the three branches of government are intended to function; understand the specific authorities that are given to national, state, and local governments; and figure out effective ways to communicate with elected officials and people in government agencies and departments. We also need to be familiar with the amendments to the constitution and, ideally, understand the context and reasons for why they were added.

Armed with such basics, the role of citizens in governing America becomes in many respects a mirror image of the role of representatives described in the previous chapter. As citizens we also need to 1) get and use good information and 2) work at understanding points of view that are different when compared to ours.

Doing those two things takes work. We all need to be open-minded, willing and ready to consider information that is new to us. Such an attitude and set of skills is critically important since we are a democracy. Our government was established to promote individual freedoms and the common good, as noted in the Preamble to the U.S. Constitution (see Appendix). We weaken America to the extent we don't honor legitimate, logical needs of others and work to balance individual needs with community needs. The fact that we live in small communities (rural areas, towns, and cities) gives us practice to better help govern larger communities (counties, states, and nation).

As is the need for our representatives, we citizens need to fight human nature tendencies, like those that reduce our interest and ability to help govern America. This means we must push aside apathy, laziness, self-centeredness, and talking only with like-minded people.

Too many Americans spend little time or energy participating in the shaping of our communities and nation. Apathy is a state of mind that occurs for many reasons: a tough life due to loss of a job, major health issues, physical and mental ability problems, or other things that keep us from involvement. But the many Americans who keep up on events affecting our nation and participate actively by attending meetings and contacting representatives shows us that most of us can discipline ourselves to participate at some level. We've just got to do it.

Many Americans *are* prepared and *get* involved with the

governing process. Many put in the kind of work needed to get their heads around good information. They go to handhelds to watch, listen, and read the news, and they monitor what's going on in their communities. I became impressed early in my tenure as a member of the Bloomington City Council with the number of residents who let me know what they think about our city. I admit to being pleasantly surprised at the number of people who watch city council meetings in person, on community cable stations, and as rebroadcasts available on the city's website.

> *Democracy—1a: government by the people;*
> *especially: rule of the majority. b: a government*
> *in which the supreme power is vested in the*
> *people and exercised by them directly or indirectly*
> *through a system of representation usually*
> *involving periodically held free elections.*
>
> *(Merriam-Webster Dictionary)*

I'm also impressed with the wide range of topics people care about—whether they're upset, pleased, seeking explanation, asking for information, giving me their ideas, or telling me what they want. I especially appreciate one-on-one dialog; it's very helpful because it improves the accuracy and quality of two-way communication.

A community of any size needs the watchful eyes of residents who communicate with their representatives and government employees. One example is an email sent to me during a major sanitary sewer replacement project in Bloomington. The email informed me that someone needed to cover the twenty-four inch pipes that were buried underground but partly exposed while waiting to be connected to other pipes yet to be added. "A child or pet could climb in there and slide down into the pipe and no one would know!"

This citizen made a very straightforward request. I thanked her and passed on the concern to our City Manager. This thoughtful and concerned person's action led to a good outcome. The contractor responded the next day by covering the open pipes. The vast majority of Americans impress me as wanting good communities and proactively engage in community building. Representatives need that kind of citizen engagement in the governing process. America needs that.

America also needs citizen involvement that monitors representatives and the issues that governing bodies address. The issues are many and far-ranging—making sure services are provided; keeping the community a safe and inviting place to live; assuring that it's a good community in which to run businesses that provide good jobs, products, and services; and being a community where activities are provided that assist residents in being successful, healthy, and happy.

We owe gratitude to the founders of America for their efforts to give us the government structure that permits us to be involved in how we deal with problems and plan a good future for ourselves as individuals and as communities and a nation. Whether as a ninth grader or at some other time in our lives, we've all been given opportunities to understand how and why America's governments operate and how we can participate.

It's up to us to play the critically important role we've been offered. We get the governing results we deserve.

Q_s

1. Who is more important in making a republic succeed— elected representatives or citizens?

2. What's on your list of ways that you participate in running our government?

3. Referendums are one way that citizens can directly vote on an issue. What are the pros and cons of referendums? What dynamics and issues come into play when a decision is to be made by potentially every voter?

Chapter 21

A Minnesota Nice Oops

**Each of us plays a role in making
relationships with others work.**

The exercise room at my local YMCA was very busy on January 1, 2014. I wondered with a smile: New Year's resolutions? Or perhaps holiday visitors still in the Twin Cities.

Despite the crowd, I had a lucky start to my Y time. I found an open locker for my jacket and street shoes and then saw that a stationary bike, my preferred workout start, was available. I was in a good mood.

After finishing my time on the bike and cleaning the seat and hand grips I headed to the area where I do a bunch of machines. I was in the middle of a fly deltoid workout when I noticed a tall, thin man about my age come toward me. He stood about six feet away, looking in different directions but regularly looking my way.

It occurred to me that he might be waiting for my machine, but I was almost done with one direction so I didn't think more about it. I wiped off the first set of handles, reset the pin to use the machine the opposite way and stood up to reverse direction.

"Can I do my other set now, work in?" he asked. "Work in" is Y lingo to encourage clients to get off a machine if they're just resting between sets. The only times I'd seen people ask to work in was when a person had been hogging the machine for a long time. I was halfway into my relatively short use of this machine and wasn't resting, so I said, "I just need to do the flip direction. It won't take long."

To my surprise, the tall guy insisted I give him the machine. I don't remember his words, but his point was clear—he had a right to do his set—now! I paused a moment, then got up and went to the next open machine. My ire was thoroughly aroused, though. I felt some heat come into my face as I started to walk away.

With too little hesitation I said with a sarcastic voice, "Do you operate on sandlot rules?" I was thinking back to when the biggest, toughest guys often ruled the kid areas where I played. His response was something like, "No. I operate on rules that say you can work in with people on a machine." Pause. "Do you live around here?" I asked. No response.

My heart rate and mental buzzing headed toward warp speed. I lost count on how many reps I had done on my grudgingly-moved-to machine.

The tall man thanked me as he finished his one set of perhaps ten reps. Sounding like a stereotyped Minnesotan, I said, "You betcha." I thought my voice sounded pretty neutral—at least that's what I aimed for. My workout continued, the adrenalin rush I'd experienced dissipating rapidly. I realized his calm "thank you" had a lot to do with my accelerating decompression.

> *"Minnesota Nice" is associated with Minnesota cul-*
> *ture, a way of being courteous, helpful, and pleasant*
> *in all situations. Someone coined the idea and now*
> *some Minnesotans feel pressured to live up to it.*

A bit later, I saw the tall man going back and forth between machines. It appeared that was his workout style—give a break to the specific muscles worked on machine *A* while working out on machine *B* and then come back to *A*. I exhaled the last of my adrenalin while drawing this tentative conclusion.

I'd never seen this guy before. Did his Dallas Cowboys T-shirt suggest he was part of the holiday visitor crowd? The norms at my Y might differ from wherever he works out, I thought.

My mind moved into its reflective mode. Why did I get *so* upset that the tall man would interrupt my workout habit? I walked into the Y rested, in a good mood. People describe me as a pretty laid-back guy. If someone like me can move so quickly to anger over a small incident, what does that say about humans in general? What does it mean for a society, for America?

I believe the answer is embedded in my early response to the situation and how the rest of my day unfolded. We have certain instincts that go back to our country's earliest days when those preservation actions were needed for the survival of the nation. Social values developed as human population exploded—values that literally enable communities to survive by figuring out how we can *mutually survive*. These values get expressed through social pressure, often times in seemingly little ways. Like what happened with me at the Y.

I started to feel *embarrassed* almost immediately after I said, "Do you operate on sandlot rules?" I didn't notice it at first. My mind was too busy being upset, I guess. But it soon became clear that the embarrassment emotion was very present. I recalled glancing around the immediate area, concerned about who might have seen and heard what happened.

The simple fact that I looked around tells me I was *concerned about public opinion.* Most of the faces at the Y that day were familiar, Y friends. I remember feeling relief that no one was staring at me. What other people think about what I do matters to me. Matters big time.

I thought about this as I drove home.

The tack I took to fix my social blunder—losing my cool with a stranger over what really was a minor disagreement—welled up from a deep storage vault of values and experience. They came from knowing I play a role in making relationships work, that I have a responsibility to be fair in my dealings with other people. They came from knowing that I make relationships worse when I get snarly. Experiences show me that *I am worse off* when that happens. I began to see this soon after it happened.

I felt very much in the spotlight almost immediately after the exchange of words. I literally needed to get back to the kind of person I want to be. I worked to do that. For the next half hour I especially bent over backwards to be polite. When I saw an elderly woman standing by a machine I wanted to use, I was extra friendly while asking if she was done. I saw someone I hadn't seen before who was wearing a Minnesota Gopher wrestling shirt and struck up a conversation about wrestling, a sport I don't follow. Driving home I was extra generous about turn-taking.

That's how a conscience works.

Brain scans are getting closer to discovering just what it is about our brains that makes us fly off the handle, act before we adequately think. But I think we know enough about our own human nature to work at shaping better behavior. We do at least to the extent that we think about "what the heck happened there!"

For me on that New Year's Day workout? I'm glad that my sixty-plus years of life experiences resulted in me feeling embarrassed. It's a good motivator. And I'm glad all the mental work that followed will result in me working harder to stifle knee-jerk reactions in the future, to buy a few seconds to simply think "hold back, Jon," and to work at sensing that I'm about to do or say something I might later regret.

I hope "tall man" discovers this chapter somehow and realizes I was the guy who made such a scene about letting him work in. Perhaps we'll reconnect some day and I'll get a chance to practice putting a relationship back on track, and likely better. It will give me a chance to repair the nick I put in the Minnesota Nice image that follows us Minnesotans wherever we go.

Q_s

1. Do you think that pushing back in situations, like my Y incident, stems from a primal instinct to protect our egos?

2. Are there times when you have said something or done something to help a friend when you sensed a situation developing where your friend and another person were starting to irritate each other? What instincts would you like to train into yourself to guide you in such a situation? Are there times when it is better to engage the friend in conversation at a different time and place?

3. How do you tell friends what you want them to do in order to help them help you avoid embarrassing yourself?

Chapter 22

Life Is Precious

Putting a value on life is not a simple decision.

Recently I saw a bumper sticker that stated "Life Is Precious." I appreciated seeing this simple reminder. I wondered if the creator of the sticker wanted me to think about life in general or to focus on pre-birth life. I wondered what the intended meaning was for the person who bought the sticker and put it on the bumper.

I was quick to agree with the message. Life is very precious. Americans seem to agree. We act out that value in many ways. Medic crews in ambulances are given the right of way. Firefighters risk their own lives, some lose them, in heroic efforts to save the life of another person. We invent machines and invest billions in research and development because consumers want to preserve or extend life.

We go to great lengths to hang on to life as age catches up with us, as we develop very serious illness, or as we suffer severe injuries because of an accident. Family members sometimes demand any and all life-saving strategies and spare no expense to keep a loved one going. We cling to life even at the point when the effects of old age mean we need an array of seemingly ever increasing and very expensive care to stay barely alive.

Of course individuals see *life-is-precious* issues from different perspectives. We're unique in how we were raised. We're affected by our life experiences. Our personalities shape our attitudes and determine how we express ourselves. We are influenced by teachings of a religion or another spirituality influence. Political party policy and campaign rhetoric sway some. No wonder we act out unique responses when confronted with *life-is-threatened* scenarios.

Unfortunately some people get revved up, impassioned, and don't talk well about the topic. At the same time, we know religious fervor and political drive are powerful in and of themselves. Mingle the two and passions run very high, and thinking logically can be overpowered. Talking about life-is-precious issues too often can get rancorous and unproductive. Americans have to somehow figure out how to increase the types of discussions that thoughtful, "what's right and not who's right" people already are having.

The array of topics is significant and weighty. The bumper sticker message "Life is Precious" seemed pretty simple when I saw it, but reflection revealed that the statement needed to be viewed in quite a few contexts.

What about warfare? We decide periodically throughout history that "something" is so important that our nation should do all it can to kill the enemy. Someone threatens our culture in some way. We want something they have. History records all kinds of reasons. How do we apply life-is-precious thinking in a warfare context?

Whatever the reason, the result of armed conflict is that

we intentionally end many precious lives. One of the most provocative examples of this paradox occurred in World War I when German soldiers started singing a Christmas carol during a Christmas Eve cease fire, and British soldiers joined in. Hours later, Christians started shooting each other again.

What about individuals that consciously decide that life is so unbearable that they want to end their own lives? How do outsiders understand someone's physical and psychological feelings of their severe and chronic pain, the inability to manage even simple personal care, or other life-isn't-worth-it-anymore thoughts? An increasing number of people have written health directives to tell medical professions how they want their end of life to be handled. How do we apply life-is-precious concepts in a context such as this?

What about the death penalty? Some of our states include this consequence for those who commit certain crimes. Each time a precious life ends by execution we are saying that a particular life isn't precious enough to preserve it. The debate lines up with one side saying executions are an effective way to deter people from committing terrible crimes. The other side argues that taking a life is morally wrong and that some executions are later determined to have punished the wrong person. The debate also grapples with which crimes, if any, require a death penalty. How do we apply life-is-precious values in this context?

What about abortion? This issue adds an extra complexity to our definition of precious life. When does life begin? Some say life begins at inception or at some other point before a child leaves the confines of the placenta. Some say life begins at birth, or the beginning of the third trimester, or when one or more organs are functional. The fact that there are people on both sides of the issue has launched many heated arguments that ultimately focus on rights of the unborn vs rights of the mother. Sometimes passions run so high that interactions are uncivil and on occasion violent. How do we apply life-is-precious thoughts in this context?

The core life-is-precious issues of such scenarios reveal why the simple statement is not as simple as it first appears. Science and societal values often point to a continuum of right and wrong instead of a clear conclusion.

There is a path that we can follow to move us toward resolution of differences about life-is-precious issues. That path begins with a realization that Americans believe life is precious. From that point we can move to the kind of problem solving that successful Americans have done since our colonial birth. We can sit across from each other, civilly listen to each other, and commit to understanding instead of seeking ways to discredit and belittle the opposition.

Interaction guidelines like those below will probably surface if a group starts by discussing dialog behaviors they want from each other. Developing participant consensus about how people like to be treated should set a positive, productive tone, especially if the group's interaction guidelines list is written down and posted in large letters in the dialog room. For example:

- Honestly seek to understand the viewpoints of people on the other side of the debate.
- Speak thoughtfully.
- Use facts that can be backed up.
- Respect others as equal members of this democracy.
- Collaboratively brainstorm and put all relevant issues and ideas on the table.

- Seek areas of agreement.
- Find ways to agree to disagree on points where consensus cannot be achieved.

Such discussions can be and have been successfully conducted. It takes wise leadership that includes thoughtful decisions about who should be in a first group, where to meet, and facilitation that makes sure that all participants have opportunities to be heard.

Sometimes bumper stickers can be really helpful—when we think about them in more than a knee-jerk way.

Q_s

1. How familiar are you with someone who is dying but lingering. What are the issues that make decisions for the individual and family or close friends difficult?

2. How do we balance the rights of the unborn with the rights of the pregnant woman?

3. We live in an era of organized terrorism. Should the United States negotiate one precious life for another, or are more precious lives saved by not rewarding hostage taking?

4. Since life is precious, how do we determine, for ourselves or on behalf of others, if there is a point when it's time to let go of earthly life? Does the answer differ for people who believe in a future life and those who don't?

Chapter 23

Stan

Get all you can out of life and then let go.

I learned a lot about how to die from an elderly friend. He let himself go in May of 2011.

Stan came into my life in a phone call. He called me to ask if the church had a media projector. I was the part-time, semi-retired director of administration at the time. Stan wanted to test out the church's equipment to make sure the DVD that he was preparing would work perfectly. The DVD was about his wife—for her memorial service—and its showing needed to come off without a hitch.

Stan told me his beloved Kate had died months before he made that phone call. He said he needed to make sure the memorial service would be just right and asked if he could meet with me. Stan showed up that afternoon. His careful planning needed to include making sure he was ready. He asked me to watch his memorial DVD as he checked out our machine. He wanted me to know about Kate and his love for her.

Stan was a character. Very intelligent. About eighty years old, he had health issues and in some ways acted as his own doctor. He read up on his ailments, his medications, his doctors.

He challenged his health care professionals. He looked beyond mainstream medicine for healthy cures that came directly from nature. He also talked with relish about other things—his career with Unisys, his military service, his children and granddaughters, the places he'd lived. At this stage in his life, however, he needed to focus on maintaining life.

He washed his store-bought apples with vinegar. He put out chunks of onion on a spare spot on his cluttered kitchen counter to absorb bad stuff in the air. He read food and beverage labels with a studied eye. Supplements were used if there was Stan-approved evidence they would help him.

Stan knew how to do wellness before wellness became a buzzword. He had a knack for it and took the time, invested the energy, to prolong his life and maintain its quality. His science-oriented, engineer's mind also understood the limits of the human body. He knew he would die. He knew how he wanted to die. He was the kind of guy who carried out plans.

"You get all you can out of life and then you let it go," he'd say. You don't prolong it with expensive treatments. You stay home just as long as you can. You're philosophical about all the what-ifs. He told me that he realized someone may find him dead on the floor, but he figured he would know when his time was up, and he had a plan ready to use when instincts told him that. With gestures of his hands he told me he'd run down the street that way, turn around and come back. And that would be it! Prolonging life, when God was ready to take you to be with Kate again, was wrong. Just let death happen.

A person tends to like the thinking of others when it resonates, when it kind of matches your own thinking. Stan took my disorganized thoughts about death and, true to his engineer's mind, organized them. Not by telling me what to do but by showing me how he was doing it.

I have a living will. I've shared it with my kids. We've talked about it. I know from the experience of witnessing the death of close relatives and friends that the circumstances that surround a person at the time of death seem never to be simple. That's why it's important for us to give our family a *feel* of how we'd like our end of life to play out.

My family knows I believe that Stan did the planning for life's end right. Keep it simple. Live right. Enjoy family and friends. Take care of yourself. Stay active. Know death is a fact of life. Avoid heroic measures. Accept the comfort of pain-control medications and techniques that are available. Let God decide when it's time for death to happen.

Q_s

1. Stan and I were almost a generation apart. He kept to himself a lot while I was socially outgoing. We came together by chance, and both of us reaped big benefits. Can people somehow seek out such relationships or do we need to wait on serendipity?

2. Stan and I met by phone, but within a few visits in his home we were confiding personal thoughts with each other as part of the wide-ranging topics we wandered into. Do we all need to be on the lookout for opportunities to start new friendships, even when we don't see how well we might connect?

3. Which is easier: talking about our end of life with family or with more distant third parties? Do you have someone in your family or a friend who helps you feel comfortable enough to talk about how you want your life to end?

Addendum: Stan died in a hospital. He wasn't there long. One of his children let me know. He didn't seem to be responsive when I talked to him and rubbed his shoulder, but perhaps there was some small awareness that evoked some memory of our many hours of conversation, debate, and giving communion to each other. When I went back two days later, his room had been cleaned up for the next patient. Perhaps Stan considered running back and forth on his quiet street but held on to life a bit too long. However, there's no question in my mind that he was at peace as he went. I imagine his beloved Kate welcomed him with a big smile.

Chapter 24

Smart Phones

How well are we managing the smart phone era?

I was several miles on my way to watch granddaughter Kate ride at a horse camp when I realized I didn't have my smart phone. Given the shortage of time to get to the stables, I traveled on without it. I figured I'd be able to survive a few hours without my phone/GPS/calendar/task list. After all, I thought, it was just a few years earlier that I made it through daily routines without even a simple cell phone.

It was a funny feeling, though. What if my daughter wanted to reach me about some change in the schedule? What if the directions I had in my head were wrong and I needed GPS help? Would I want to check my calendar to see if I entered an event that my drive-time-thoughts recalled? What if someone really needed to reach me; might they worry or be irritated because I didn't answer the phone?

How we connect with people has changed dramatically in just a few years. It's like the smart phone has become a human organ, an appendage to the brain. We communicate via text, tweets, emails, Facebook, Snapchat, and the parade of new ways to socialize. We've moved away from voice contact. I've discovered it's pretty useless to ask people during an email or text exchange to give me a call—almost everyone ignores the request and continues the *contorted conversation* through the hand held.

I've decided I need to develop strategies to cope. One thought is to periodically go a day without my phone, so I remember how, the old-fashioned way, to communicate with other humans, find my way, keep track of my schedule, and manage my to-do list. I figure I'll be less stressed when losing or forgetting my phone if I've had practice going without. I might be the hero if everyone's smart device became worthless in a disaster—I could step up to show them how to function without their phones.

I certainly don't want to become so dependent on my smart phone that I freak out without it. Freaking out means losing the ability to problem solve and find solutions that can avoid chaos.

I'm not predicting that our dependence on ever-evolving handhelds will lead to a catastrophic end to the planet. Most smart phone users are mentally nimble enough that loss of use is confined to annoyance and irritation. Americans are generally good about making do when something they depend on, like a cell phone, isn't available. We're improvisers.

How I respond to forgetting or losing my smart phone is an individual thing. It's my own problem if I don't have a backup plan. Every one of us deserves to learn a lesson once in a while if we're careless about leaving our phone in restaurants, don't backup information, get too cavalier about changing passwords, etc. etc.

But the smart phone takeover of our society is more than an individual issue. It's a cultural issue. We've become so dependent on them for so many purposes that they—physical objects—have increasingly become our life focus on a daily basis. Smart phone use has dramatically affected how we use our time and how we relate to others. My workout trainer told me he's designing workout strategies to reduce physical problems that, he's convinced, come from poor posture during the long periods of time some clients are on the phone. The impact of smart phones is pervasive—virtually everyone older than a young child has one.

What does this mean for community, what does this mean for our culture?

I don't ride a bus or travel in a plane often, but I have used both enough times to notice that there are fewer conversations among people thrown together as they go from point A to point B. There's less connectedness in our nation. I eat in restaurants at least once a week and regularly see people interfacing with their phones more than they talk to others at their table. There's less connectedness in my community. I experience less each-other-focused conversation within my own home and when I'm with relatives at family events. Phone use is nudging out face-to-face social interaction in America.

Cultural changes, like the invention and expanded use of smart phones, sometimes build momentum like that of a boulder given a push at the top of a mountain. Smart phones are coming at us like boulders. Even old timers like me like them. They truly are fun to use. They save me time. I can get the news, from many sources, in a hurry and with ease.

Same goes for researching something I want to know more

about. No need to trek to a library like we needed to twenty years ago. No more dependence on a desktop or laptop computer like just a few years ago. And what about the Pokémon Go craze of 2016? My gosh, we're way beyond the science fiction two-way wrist radio of Dick Tracy cartoon strips I followed in the 1950s. I'm living the imaginary future of my childhood!

Smart phones are obviously here to stay. Like any cultural boulder-coming-down-the-mountain change, it's up to us to manage the boulder's route and limit the unintended damage it does along the way. Will the smartphone-boulder damage our sense of family, our sense of community and nation? Can we steer the handheld changes so they help us connect with people we might not otherwise connect to? Do they, can they, promote healthy relationships in some way *even if* we're not face-to-face?

How will the pros and cons of smart phones sort out, and will they make us proud about how we managed their impact on America? The rush of new wireless devices coming at us is revolutionizing our lives. Used wisely, smart phone type devices give us the opportunity to make our nation better— more efficient, better informed, more connected, a stronger democracy—if we're smart in how we use them.

Q_s

1. One dinner hour I noticed a teenage male and another person I guessed was a father in a restaurant booth barely eight feet away. Occasional glances in their direction

indicated smart phones consumed a lot of their time. What options might explain why they spent so little time looking and talking to each other? In what ways might smart phones be a positive factor in their relationship? In what ways a negative?

2. In what ways do smart phones increase people connectedness? How/when do these devices reduce the quality of relationships and increase disconnectedness?

3. Nomophobia (the fear or anxiety of not having mobile phone contact) is a word that is showing up in new dictionaries. Do you think scientific study will confirm that such a fear can actually reach a phobia level? Have you ever had a panic attack when you can't find your phone? How do you feel if you're someplace, like in a forest, where your phone doesn't work?

Chapter 25

Value of Work

**We build stronger communities when we
honor and fairly value all types of work.**

The Oracle of Omaha, aka Warren Buffet (known for wise
opinions and decisions), got a lot of press a few years ago for
his *New York Times* op-ed piece advocating tax reform. The
attention-grabber, spread by all forms of media, was when he
said his secretary paid a higher tax rate than he did. He noted
that, thanks to tax breaks and loopholes, the ultra-rich are
richer than ever before.

A billionaire making such a statement was both refresh-
ing and disturbing to me. Buffet's comments set off extensive
chatter and arguments about the fairness of the American tax
system. It was certainly not the first time that the topic was
making headlines. I wondered if this time the issue would have
staying power and lead to a healthy national conversation that
might produce a shift toward greater equity in quality of life
for Americans.

I chose to stay out of the messy, ultimately unproductive
furor, but it did arouse some reflection about income disparity
in our nation.

There are lots of ways to make a living, lots of different work to be done. That's a good thing. There are lots of things that need doing! Consider the things needed for an individual to live, a community to survive, and ideally for all to thrive. But there's a phenomenon about the human being that complicates that simple concept. We tend to think more highly about people in some occupations while looking down our noses at those who do other jobs. That's a reality that messes around with feelings of human self-worth, not to mention negative outcomes for the well-being of our nation.

It's difficult to study the value of work without comparing one type against another, which leads us too quickly into making impulsive, self-serving value judgments. How valuable is it to have someone pick up our garbage, help us save money, run large and small companies, take care of us when we're sick, build or maintain our living quarters, educate us, entertain us, or govern us? Can we, should we, create a list that ranks every specific job according to its value to America? I think not, not without a lot of subjectivity, without consciously or subconsciously being self-serving.

The exercise would be interesting though! Some jobs are high profile and provide high pay, some are less so. I'm sure we'd be at least subconsciously influenced by current work compensation; people tend to assume that people who make more money have earned it because somehow they're worth it. But I believe that during our effort to make that ranked list, we'd decide that pay and prestige can lead to warped thinking about which jobs are *truly* more valuable to us, to our quality of life.

Someone might make a comment that they're very glad they don't have to haul away their own garbage, much less the garbage of others. I can imagine someone else chiming in with, "And there's no way I'd want to drive the bulldozer that pushes the smelly stuff into piles or work in the garbage incineration facility. Can you imagine what it would be like to have the job of fixing a conveyer belt that stopped carrying garbage into the incinerator?"

These and others are not prestigious jobs, but many of us would agree we're glad someone is willing to do them. So how do we rank them on the Value to Society list?

If we continued our ranking efforts, perhaps our list-making discussion would stray into talk about how work has changed over time. Doing hard work has been extolled throughout our nation's history. From early on, work in farming, blacksmithing, cooking, making dairy products, doing laundry, or operating a store meant hard physical labor. The work ethic in the old days was equated with muscle, sweat, fifty to sixty or more hours per week, sometimes seven-day work weeks, going to bed bone tired—for both genders and whether free or slave.

By the middle of the twentieth century, however, electricity, machines, and other inventions ended the need for so much physical labor. "White collar" and "blue collar" workers became the way we classified people at work. Each group included some who derided the other side.

I remember such an atmosphere while I was a kid. I was old enough to notice as the criteria to evaluate different types of work shifted from *physically demanding* work toward *soft jobs*. I remember hearing "sissy" from one side and "dummy" from the other. You were a sissy if you did soft jobs; your IQ was questioned if you did brawny work. Neither stereotype, of course, is true. And such stereotyping does not create the kind of environment that encourages people to realize that *our nation needs both* white collar and blue collar workers.

The way people work to be able to provide for daily needs continues to evolve. I'm glad somebody does stuff I don't want to do. I'm glad others understand how to do things I can't do—make things at a nano-sized level, design internet security tools, design the mini-computers that do all kinds of things, engineer sky scrapers, and construct light weight bullet proof vests. Also I am very appreciative that I can call on someone who knows how, and is willing, to clean up my basement if the sewer line backs up. I appreciate that every Tuesday my garbage and recycling is picked up.

I've worked in a variety of organizations, for-profit and not-for-profit businesses. Across the board I saw income inequity based on society's view of how valuable each employee was to the organization. I saw highly paid supervisors who were propped up by people lower on the organizational chart, often women, who were paid much less but provided critically important value. I saw guys during my summer railroad job in the 1960s smirk when a cocky new supervisor told them to do something they knew from experience wouldn't work. I remember thinking pay should have been equal for both job types—if not inverted.

The pecking order of *more-valued* and *less-valued* workers in an organization can be really messed up sometimes!

Do we have the knowledge, will, courage, and skill to change the institutional and societal views that value some work much more than other work? Can we move the norm to compensate individuals for the value they provide our nation rather than because of their gender, skin color, or other characteristics? How do we make compensation fair, not just a pecking order system developed by those in charge?

We need many oracles in America to help us broaden our understanding of the value that *all* American workers bring to the table to make our country work.

The effort will be worth it! When we value all types of work in a manner that is thoughtful, fair, and more than opinion-based, we build a stronger nation. When we value, honor, and fairly compensate people in all types of work, the United States becomes more successful and secure.

Q*s*

1. What are the subtle and not so subtle ways we communicate "you're less important than me"?

2. In what way do parents, business leaders, and other organization leaders genuinely communicate that a person is valued?

3. In what ways are businesses affected when employees believe the company compensation is significantly out of balance with their personal perception of fairness?

Chapter 26

Enabled Society?

**Strong nations and strong individuals find
solutions to problems within themselves.**

Early in my teen years I occasionally spent time with a friend
at his family's cabin on a lake near Detroit Lakes, MN. One
summer Larry got outriggers and a small sail to attach to their
family canoe—paddling was too slow we had decided. We
were horrible canoe sailors! I remember one day when it was
my turn to stretch out under the thwarts, providing ballast
and staying out of the way of the rigging, while Larry tried to
figure out the sail and rudder. I didn't drown, but came close a
couple of times!

We gave up on dreams of flying across Big Detroit Lake in a
canoe. I don't think the sailing canoe idea flew well elsewhere
either; I haven't seen one in a long time. As I look back on the
experience, I do recall *what we didn't do*. We didn't complain
to anyone. We simply moved on with life realizing we tried
to do something we weren't trained to do or weren't naturally
good at. I'm not proud that I didn't keep trying until we mas-
tered the darn thing, but I do feel good about the fact that we
didn't blame someone else for our failure.

We didn't think once about bringing the equipment back to the dealer to demand our money back for "this crappy design and unsafe product." We didn't think about suing anyone about the bruises we got when going overboard or getting wacked on the head by the rigging as it swung wildly.

It was a different time. Today it seems we have moved away from how two young teenagers saw their world in the late '50s. Too many of us have become complainers and blamers. We'd rather find someone else to be responsible for things in our life that didn't go right. Too many of us expect that someone will take care of us so we don't have to. Blaming others and shirking responsibility have become so pervasive that it can be said we are a society that enables.

Truth be told, our enabling tendency goes far beyond the entitlement programs that get the finger pointing: welfare, affordable care, Medicare, Medicaid, and Social Security. Consider how some businesses have been enabled, including those who now feel entitled. Too many seek tax incentives, tax shelters, or protective tariffs. Some reap big benefits from government trade officials who help them get business. Some get amazingly high income when doing work for governments. Yes, some businesses have been enabled instead of fully standing on their own feet.

Some companies now play the game to get handouts. Too many business owners say they will locate their business in a state or city that gives them the biggest chunk of taxpayer money. They promise jobs, an improved tax base, and the pride that goes with having their company or their sports team or their big name status come to your community or state. But that is often more a negotiating ploy than it is a verifiable taxpayer return on investment. I am one of the Minnesotans who still remembers Northwest Airlines (NWA) getting taxpayer subsidies to locate a maintenance facility in northern Minnesota. NWA got their benefits. The facility was built, but taxpayers never got the promised full return on investment. NWA is no more; its successor has its corporate headquarters in another state.

A strong nation, its citizens and businesses, doesn't look elsewhere for help unless it's absolutely necessary. Strong nations and strong individuals find solutions to problems within themselves. We need to acknowledge that too many Americans are not emphasizing those habits like we have done in periods of greater success.

We can get back to being a "we can do it ourselves" dominated culture. Yes, we need to make changes in policy and law—overhauling, for example, how we do social services so the programs meet real needs and don't enable. We also need to change how governments subsidize businesses, so taxpayer money doesn't simply add income to corporations and investors. People start businesses and invest in them knowing that there is a risk of poor performance and ultimate failure. Investment brokers tell us the greater the risk, the greater the potential returns. It's not a citizen's responsibility to reduce those businessperson's risks, unless return of taxpayer money over a reasonable timeline is truly guaranteed.

It's not just a national level issue. We need, every one of us needs, to think through how we live our lives and how we influence each other toward self-sufficiency. There is no more important way we do this than in how we raise our children and the values we pass along to them. We hear today about the negative effects of helicopter parenting—parents who too often swoop in and fix problems for their children, including young adult children, before even giving them the chance to solve it themselves. We've all seen how toddlers, after taking a fall, learn how okay or bad off they are by detecting adult responses to their misfortune. Some adults react with an immediate flurry of "oh, you poor thing" while rushing to them as though they're about to call 911. Tone of voice and the look in the face of an adult communicate so much to a young child.

When a child sees in the adult that a minor scrape is catastrophic, there will be a tendency to see other problems as bigger than they really are. The same toddlers who are rescued on a playground by overly alarmed parents may expect someone to rescue them over and over again in life, when they take tumbles of all sorts in school, on the job, or in relationships. This mind set becomes a breeding ground for persons to *habitually* think they cannot solve their own problems and then decide they need help. Such people have no chance to figure out how to resolve huge problems.

Consider a different response by an adult to a child's scraped knee. Ponder the results of a calm face and voice accompanied with matter of fact actions that tell the child a different life lesson. "Whoops! You tripped there, didn't you? Let's take a look at your knee," followed by the use of basic first aid and a dose of attitude: "Are you ready to go back to play now?"

People generally find that they feel better about themselves when they rarely ask for or expect help.

There are of course times when individuals really need assistance, need to lean on friends or family members to help. Life throws us curves sometimes, such as personal tragedies of any sort or situations when life seems unbearable because of a horrible accident or a devastating health problem or drug addiction (legal or illicit). There *are* times when large numbers of people need the help of a community instead of going it alone, especially in times of natural disasters, such as a flood or extended drought; tornados; fires; and acts of terrorism.

It's a matter of direction and degree. We're better off, as individuals and as a nation, when our goal and our efforts are to take care of ourselves instead of *first* looking for someone else to take care of us. We're better off when we assume responsibility. We're better off looking at failed plans to sail a canoe as learning experiences rather than as reasons to complain and blame.

*Q*s

1. Did those who lived through the Great Depression, truly a great generation, unwittingly set the stage for an enabling trend by wanting to protect their children/ grandchildren from going through the difficult times they experienced?

2. How do you determine when a friend or family member *really* needs help? How do you decide if helping them would instead weaken them in a way that actually makes their lives ultimately worse?

3. How in the heck do we develop reasonable county, city, state, and national polices that balance helping people in true need with fostering an attitude that says, "I can and need to take care of myself"?

4. Writing this chapter flashed me back to a book read to me as a young child: *The Little Engine that Could.* It's still in my neighborhood public library! What other children's books help our little ones learn to live with an "I can do it" attitude?

Chapter 27

Getting Off the Elevator

**We all are responsible for the race relations
environment of our nation.**

It was after 9:00 p.m. one night in the early 1990s when I
headed to the elevator in Duluth's Central Administration
Building to head home. I had an office there for two years as
the Social Studies Curriculum Specialist, a position given the
responsibility to coordinate K-12 social studies for the school
district. The position gave me an opportunity to get some variety in my professional life.

As I heard the elevator approach my floor, I walked closer
to the door. I was eager to get home. The door started to open
and I saw a custodian with a mop and bucket. I took a quick
step backward.

There was no question then, and no question now, that my
step backward was instinctive. The man was African American. I was immediately embarrassed.

I'm a gregarious person, quick to engage in conversation even with strangers. But that night, at that moment,
my personality and my very being were driven by instinct.
I say skin color and cultural differences simply describe

variations—we're all humans. I mean it when I say such things, and I'm pretty good at living what I say. I try not to be racist.

But that night, at that instant, I knew I was. I hated the feeling. I was embarrassed. But it was there. So deeply engrained that I know it welled up in me from someplace very deep within me.

I'm familiar with issues about racism. I was in college in the 1960s when many voices were raised and actions taken as America struggled to understand and respond to racism and sexism. The Civil Rights Movement was an encouraging indication that many Americans wanted people of all skin colors to benefit from the lofty goals recorded in a variety of America's history documents.

During the 1978–1980 school years I spent another stint out of the classroom, in that case as co-director of the district's Ethnic, Cultural, Non-Sex-Bias Center. We conducted three-day workshops for classroom teachers on racism and sexism. We also operated an Elementary Secondary Education Act program we called Recapturing Our Heritage. We recruited and coordinated volunteers from a variety of ethnic and racially diverse populations to go into classrooms to share their cultural heritage with students.

In short, I had been steeped in the issues of racism. And yet there I was that night, impulsively communicating to a total stranger, a quiet, slight man, that I was afraid when I saw him. There was absolutely no rational reason to be afraid of this person. There was no way I could explain that quick step backward except to acknowledge that I somehow had racist instincts.

I have no idea what the certainly-not-threatening man saw on my face. I don't remember if I uttered any sound. I don't recall if I recovered enough to say "hi" or engage in small talk like we gregarious people do.

The damage was done in two seconds. I never saw the man again.

What I remembered as I drove home, and still remember decades later, was the look on his face and what his body communicated to me. His face was sad, perhaps no more sad than throughout most of his time in our 90 percent white city. Some faces express sadness by forced habit.

I also recalled how his body slumped ever so slightly as he sensed my communication to him. All I could think of was how likely this slender, fifty-something man must have felt— being stereotyped will never end.

I am one who wants to understand, to empathize, to fix. And yet, despite the retreats on racism that I'd attended during my mid-60s college years and later teaching years, despite the workshops I'd helped facilitate for teacher colleagues, the professional growth classes I'd taken, the conversations I'd had with friends who happened to be people of color—despite all that, I instinctively stepped back that night when the elevator door opened.

The incident happened several decades ago. I'm frustrated that I haven't fully kicked the racism that lurks in me. I'm cautious when I'm with people of color that I don't know, I'm not as natural as I want, need, to be. I'm making progress. I have found a comfort level with a few African Americans. Too few. We are very open with each other, disagree about some things, and stay friends. Funny how I'd think having a friend I can argue with makes me feel so good.

We all are responsible for the race relations environment of our nation. How we interact as individuals in our local communities determines the national reality. Each one of us simply has to do our part to help our nation act out the noble words of the Founding Fathers when they signed their names to "all people are created equal," and we all "are endowed by our Creator with certain unalienable rights, among them life, liberty, and the pursuit of happiness."

I have a tendency to instinctively reject simple explanations and simple answers to weighty questions, but on the topic of race relations I've come to the conclusion that a very simple goal is spot on: We need to think one-on-one. Not easy to achieve, but easier to get my head around and helpful in giving me focus, helpful in giving me direction in how I can do my part.

> *America will be better off someday when we earthlings think and talk about everyone as fellow humans.*

What I need to do, what we all need to do, is to engage proactively with *persons* who grew up in cultural trappings different than ours. We need to push ourselves to experience life together, at a personal level. We need to prepare ourselves to do that until we are able to shape how we start these personal interactions with a blank slate that is free of preconceptions and prejudgments.

We need lots of those experiences—many dialogs, many hang out withs, many exchanges of baring our souls about simple and heavy topics. It starts with one person we kinda know. We expand our horizons by offering ourselves to another individual. And another. And another.

Doing so until we learn how to do "I'm really getting to know you" stuff. Doing so until we become comfortable in launching such relationships. Doing so until we stop looking at another human being in a society-induced stereotypical way. Doing so until we're okay with accepting that we don't have to agree on some things, that we are different in a *few* ways.

Doing all this until doing so becomes a habit. I know from personal experience that we will be enriched; there will be rewards that encourage us along the mountain climb to support us in casting off old habits and replacing them with much, much better habits. We'll then be more skilled and motivated to remove the institutional racism throughout our society that is both morally wrong and harmful to our nation.

By *really getting to know* persons who we perceive as being different from us, we'll go a long way toward understanding why we, as individuals, do stuff like stepping back when elevator doors open because we see someone who simply looks different than ourselves. There will be lots of bonuses coming out of our efforts, for us and for our nation.

Q_s

1. What helps you become more open to getting to know, genuinely understand, another person you don't know very well?

2. The human being is very self-centered. How do we learn to see ourselves as others see us?

3. Do you suppose we'll be less prone to prejudge when we discover that others see us differently than how we see ourselves?

4. How we interact with other humans is arguably most real as a one-on-one dynamic. The world seems increasingly to de-emphasize and reduce face-to-face time. How do we get to know another person without being physically together?

Chapter 28

Bull Nose Ring

**We need to realize when we're being
"led by the nose."**

Outdoor life has always had a magnetic pull on me. I remember as a child wanting to stay outside to play longer than I was permitted. I loved visits to the farms of Iowa relatives. Farmers did outdoors stuff! Riding tractors, riding on the hay wagons, and helping with chores felt so good I thought that one day I would be a farmer. Perhaps that's why a farm animal image came to mind when I read about the petition drive that a Nebraska Target employee started in November 2011.

Target had just announced plans to open their stores at midnight on Thanksgiving in order to get an early start on Black Friday. The petition asked Target to reconsider the change and allow workers to spend Thanksgiving Day with family and friends—instead of at work. Target's response: "We need to match our competition." A true statement of course, but something didn't feel right.

As I followed this story I recalled a childhood conversation I had with Uncle Vic after I saw a bull with a ring in his nose and asked him why that was. I don't remember my uncle's explanation word for word, but I somehow came to understand that the ring was put in a bull's nose to control him, to get him to do whatever a person holding the rope attached to the ring wanted.

A powerful image. It got me wondering, thinking about how we humans are sometimes led around, somehow pulled into doing things that we don't want to do. I wondered why people would shop on a holiday like Thanksgiving. It seems kind of odd since on holidays we tend to look forward to a few hours of celebrating, being together with family and friends, and getting out of the hectic frenzy that seems to dominate American life. Is being pulled into frenzied shopping amidst pushing and shoving crowds really what we want to be doing on Thanksgiving?

The reality is that the vast majority of us are regularly, not just at Thanksgiving, being controlled quite effectively by glitzy ads on TV, on our many electronic devices, before movies start in theaters, and on mass transit. We're pulled into wanting more stuff, needing to have more than other people whom we see as competitors.

Like a bull with a ring in his nose, we often are pulled in the direction that American businesses want. We are seduced, wanting to look like movie stars, be cool like sports heroes, or lose weight just like "those average people" who look so much better in the "after picture." We go where we're pulled because we seemingly can't resist. We shop midnight specials that mess up our sleep habits, even pitch a tent or curl up in a sleeping bag on the cement in front of a store so that we *might* get one of a half dozen super deals. Some of us do such things even when it's very cold outside. We may even take a risk by skipping work.

Obviously, American consumers don't have rings in their noses hooked to ropes controlled by storeowners. Not literally. But in a real sense we are pulled into buying on impulse, buying stuff and later wondering if we really needed it. We are pulled into dishonoring family by leaving them early to shop on Thanksgiving Day. Good for us? Good for American society? A good legacy to pass on?

Most Americans, even big business executives, would probably agree that Thanksgiving and other holidays should be a time to stop the rat race of life for a day to be thankful—to spend quality time with family, kick back and relax, worship with our faith community, or serve meals to people who don't get three squares a day. But neither the corporate decision makers nor we the people have taken an effective stand to insist "holidays are an important rest stop for America."

It took a low echelon Target employee to risk some form of employer retaliation in order to say, "Enough is enough." Good for him.

I get it—that it's bottom-line smart for a retail business to take advantage of the low hanging fruit that's so tantalizing out there during what we've collectively decided is the biggest sales season of the year. But I also wonder—wonder if we've gone too far, if as consumers we've let ourselves get sucked in to changing too much about us, about our society.

Sometimes change creeps up on us, into us, and we don't realize what we're doing to ourselves. As a child I remember hearing my parents become agitated as they talked about how the Blue Laws that closed most businesses on Sunday were eroding. These laws protected values we put into practice back then. The message I picked up as a kid was that these laws were honoring the importance of religious life, as well as a common sense realization that we needed a day of rest. I had learned as a kid that the Ten Commandments said Sunday was to be kept sacred and be a day to catch our breath. For our family, that meant we would go to church, return home, have a special meal, and have leisure time the rest of the day—spend time with friends, do a special family activity, watch television, take a nap.

Then, as now, only a percentage of the population worshipped on Sunday. But then, as not so much now, it was generally acknowledged and respected that the human body/ mind/spirit needed to take a day off once in a while. One day a week seems about right.

It's been decades since I heard anyone talk about Sunday Blue Laws, perhaps because the few that remain are only for a short list of business types. Did the foresight of my parents and others foretell the problems running rampant now? We hear how stress contributes to a number of physical and mental health problems. Perhaps with a day of rest more people would be healthier because they could simply relax, or they could exercise by taking a walk, going to the beach, joining a Sunday sports league, or some other physical activity. Heaven knows our obesity prone culture today needs to exercise more, and doing exercise stuff on our day off would be a good thing.

> *Blue laws, also known as Sunday laws, are laws*
> *designed to restrict or ban some or all Sunday*
> *activities for religious reasons, particularly to*
> *promote the observance of a day of worship or rest.*
>
> (Wikipedia)

For me, I am glad the Target employee stuck his neck out because I believe he gave America a wakeup call, to step back and evaluate what we're doing to ourselves. It certainly and absolutely is not just Target. The commercialization, the fostering of materialism that has come to dominate our culture, is rampant. We are at a critical point. We need to think about what we are doing to our society and figure out ways we can take a variety of actions that elevate holidays and one day a week to celebrate life, nurture our spiritual side, cut ourselves some slack, and step off the rat race wheel.

We need to ask ourselves if we have a ring in our nose. We need to wonder if we have let ourselves become controlled in ways that aren't good for us as individuals or as a nation.

*Q*s

1. Many people stay away from Black Friday like it was the Black Plague. Why do you or someone you know stay away from such good deal specials?

2. For you, what's okay and what's not okay about stores being open on holidays?

3. Is the burden of working on holidays a classism issue? In your observation, what income level works on holidays? On Sundays?

4. There is still residue from Sunday Blue Laws, either through legislation still on the books or due to cultural habit or pressure. For example, most office buildings are closed both weekend days. What are other examples?

5. Do you have a bull nose ring in your nose?

Chapter 29

Schools Like Corporations?

**Can schools and businesses help each other
while honoring their unique roles in America?**

A thirty-something teacher and I struck up a conversation as
we walked to our cars after a meeting one evening in 2012. It
was a penetratingly cold November night but it was the conversation that provided the real chill.

Anna is an elementary school special education teacher. We
educators have a bond so it came naturally to ask, "How is your
school year going?" Her response opened a floodgate. She said
she didn't know how much longer she could stay in her chosen
profession. As she talked about the changes in education during
the years since she began her teaching career, it became obvious
that she was worn out, disillusioned, and frustrated.

As the flow of frustration coming through the floodgate
slowed, I asked if a big part of her frustration was society's
emphasis on standardized testing. She said that was a part of it,
but there was more. Education has become a numbers game,
and how teachers relate to their students is devalued. Instead
of focusing on building a friendly, positive learning environment, teachers are under pressure to squeeze out more from

scarcer dollars, handle larger class sizes, and always "get those test scores up."

She said a changing atmosphere is enveloping "school"—a businesslike tone that infiltrates student-teacher relationships. Anna used a phrase that stuck in my mind as I drove home. She said schools now feel more like corporations.

I worked professionally with kids for over thirty-five years as a youth director, teacher, and school principal, and I still work with young people occasionally as a volunteer. In all of these roles it's become very obvious to me that *how I relate to young people* is critical to my ability to help them get along with other people, recognize the importance of attitude, understand the process of problem solving, and be aware of the need to continue learning academic content covered in school classrooms— the stuff needed in daily life, throughout life.

Developing a relationship with students happens one student at a time. Sure, how a teacher manages the classroom as a whole is a critical part of that picture. But it's the little things that happen one-on-one that seals the deal. One-on-one conversations, for example, about how to do a math problem gives the comfort level students thrive on when feeling that an adult will help them—at their pace of grasping understanding.

Schools don't meet their potential when adult-young person interactions are one-way-fits-all. Children have different learning styles. They have varied home and parenting situations. The egos of some young humans are especially fragile and develop best when a caring adult gives them personally delivered support and guidance.

Corporations are perhaps obviously different from K-12 schools. They market to segments of a population; public schools are called upon to serve all children in their neighbor-hoods, not just select segments. Corporations need to teach employees by using adult learning styles; schools need to use a range of teaching methods that fit the range of brain devel-opment stages that occur as students progress from pre-school through high school. Corporations measure success based on financial bottom lines; schools base success on outcomes that are subject to the sometimes changing whims of public elected officials. And some school objectives, such as developing inquiring minds and learning how to get along with others, are sometimes very difficult to measure in a way that the vocally critical may demand.

I'm aware that various school-business partnerships develop with positive outcomes. I'm impressed with several high powered efforts going on in Minnesota today to give effective support to low income students. Such successes stem from thoughtful collaboration and genuine efforts to understand how business ideas can actually help teachers and their schools get better results. On the flip side, some businesses appreciate and learn from, for example, the people management skills many teachers demonstrate.

The rubber hits the road in K-12 schools whenever and wherever teacher-student interactions occur. Many teachers are drawn to the teaching profession because they deeply care about kids and genuinely want to help them mature and develop lifelong skills, as well as learn the academic stuff. Hav-ing experienced over three decades of being a public school educator, I empathize with the Anna's in today's schools.

It's appropriate for Americans to keep a watchful eye on how our schools operate, to expect good results, and to monitor the return on our tax money investment. Doing that well requires that we take the time, expend the effort to get a real sense of the dynamics that occur in the diverse-in-so-many-ways students that Anna and colleagues across the country must manage.

Business models that produce outcomes that make corporations happy simply do not transfer to the essentially different outcomes that K-12 schools must seek—helping individual students succeed. Key elements of good education models are not mirror images of good corporate models.

Teaching is a demanding profession, and one of America's most important. We can't afford to lose great teachers like Anna. A democracy cannot survive without a well-educated citizenry. We need to figure out the kind of support that keeps sharp, caring, motivated teachers like Anna in America's classrooms.

Q_s

1. Most Americans have experienced the student side of K-12 schools, but only a few have become teachers. How can adults who aren't teachers get a reasonably true, comprehensive understanding of what it is like to be a public school classroom teacher?

2. Public and private K-12 schools in America play major roles in the lives of students for at least seven hours a weekday during the school year—more when before and after school activities are included. What does your list of what schools should accomplish with America's children look like?

3. In what ways do you think business leaders can best assist schools in their efforts to help students become successful individuals, prepare for work life, and be good citizens?

4. What do you do to support teachers you perceive to be good for America's children?

Chapter 30

Mission Statements in a Democracy

**Defining a group's purpose is hard work
but worth the effort.**

As an active member of various schools and organizations over many years, I've been involved too many times in developing a mission statement. It is a tough job! Discussions about a group's mission can go on so long and get so contentious that I'm not eager to volunteer for such efforts. They fascinate me though, so I rarely pass up an opportunity to take a minute to read one when I see it.

While attending a panel presentation one afternoon in the Richfield (MN) Public Schools District complex, I noticed the District's mission statement in a framed document on a wall. It read, *The mission of the Richfield Public Schools is to prepare all learners for success in a changing world by developing their knowledge and abilities within a climate of mutual trust and respect.*

"Not bad," I thought. Mission statements are supposed to be short, to the point and summarize the gist of why an organization exists. This one does a darn good job.

The session that drew me to the room that displayed the statement had a sign-in and social time that I hadn't planned on, so I succumbed to my tendency to ponder. I picked the statement apart, imagining the fervent frustration those drafting it probably experienced.

Success for all learners. Hmm, if America's democracy is going to thrive, we need successful schools! If *every* learner is successful—well, imagine how great the United States could be.

In a changing world. It certainly is a changing world. We do need Americans to be adaptable, to be ready and open to understanding change, to be prepared to decide whether to readily accept or be cautious about a change, and to take part in managing changes.

Develop knowledge. Excuse me, but hasn't that been a goal of education in our country since the Founders said residents in a democracy needed it? It's hard to imagine a democracy being successful if "we the people" are illiterate. We need developed minds—problem solving, creative, caring minds—capable of processing the incredibly diverse and voluminous information that would otherwise overwhelm us.

Develop abilities. A person needs a wide range of abilities to make literally anything happen in governments, businesses, families, and organizations. Kids need to develop their mental, physical, and emotional abilities as their brains mature. Students enter schools with different levels of skill competence, different inherited and home-developed traits. Schools have a mission to bring all up to speed. Each student must, and can, learn how to develop *new* abilities, as well as improve the abilities they already have. Such givens create a challenge for schools, a challenge we all must tackle.

Within a climate. Yes! The environment of any place affects how people feel, act, and learn. It's good that Richfield schools work to provide a climate that is conducive to learning.

A climate of trust. Whatever our ages, we work most eagerly when we don't detect deviousness, don't feel taken advantage of, and are permitted to function on a level playing field. Trust is a critically important element anywhere people interact, especially in a school environment where young minds are in such a formative stage.

A climate of respect. Feeling respected and cared about propels humans to put effort toward achievement, to strive for success. Such an environment creates optimism and a "can do" student body. School-age individuals, young minds going through key formative years, bloom more fully and produce better results when they feel they are worthy, respected.

Okay, I caught myself thinking, I'll accept the next time I'm asked to help write a mission statement. I won't expect it to be easy. It's hard to put purpose into a twenty-three-word statement like the Richfield people did. Schools are especially complex places. Each staff member, parent, and student will have pet ideas; there will be hidden agendas; taxpayers will always ask, "What will it cost to do all this nice sounding stuff?" Putting your life's work into a couple dozen words is a difficult task. Merging the personal thoughts of many into a few words in a consensus building process? Whew, that's really tough!

But it's a good thing to do. It is good to get that focus, to go through all the effort of defining goals. Groups that struggle to distill what they strive to accomplish in a collaborative way remind themselves of their purpose. In some ways the biggest benefit I've taken away from such work sessions stems from the dialog, the debate, the sharing of passion that we experience as we work together. Even the arguing reveals that we care about why we come to work.

Living in a democracy gives us the opportunity to set direction for what we want to achieve, who we want to be, in groups of any size. The hard work of reaching consensus is not easy but it's what makes us a democracy. The outcomes make the hard work worthwhile.

Q_s

1. Americans argue sometimes about what schools should focus on, what their purpose should be. What phrases would you include in the mission statement of schools in your community? How well would your list satisfy the variety of people who live in your community?

2. Who should participate in developing mission statements in your work place or any other group you are part of?

3. What do you think about pulling your family members together to talk about the mission, purpose, or goals (whatever you call the outcomes) for your family? How do you figure out when children are developed enough, mentally and emotionally prepared enough, to participate?

Chapter 31

Gender Roles

**Changing cultural perceptions of gender roles
is an ongoing process.**

I recently watched a thirty-something dad in our neighbor-hood pushing his two kids in a jogging stroller. As I waved to them, I thought this man is doing what used to be women's work. Such a scene is no longer a surprise. It's become increasingly common for American fathers to spend a lot of time with their kids. Doing things for them. Doing things with them.

I was that kind of father myself when my children were born, going with the cultural transition flow already started in the 1970s. I attended birthing classes, was in the delivery room, and, when back home, changed diapers and took my turn in getting up with them in the middle of the night.

Male involvement with their children changed rapidly in America. Gender roles were still very sharply defined when I reached a double digit age in the mid-'50s. My dad and mom were pretty typical. Dad saw himself as the breadwinner, the lawn mowing guy, and head of the household. Mom was the homemaker, doing the cleaning, laundry, and dishes in addition to taking care of my sisters and me. She never learned to drive, and, at least in front of us, deferred to my father when decisions were made.

That all seemed about right as I grew up in that home. I didn't see many adults in my community who didn't fit those roles. Men and women who were different were, well, seen as "different," perceived as a bit of an oddity. I didn't hear anybody label them non-conformists or accuse them of messing with the social and moral fabric of society—nothing as radical as that.

As for my role-taking, I periodically overheard people say that I was *all boy*. I figured out that when adults used that descriptor they meant I liked playing with trucks, being outside a lot, getting dirty, playing sports, and getting into a little trouble (like sneaking into the county fairgrounds a few blocks away to play cops and robbers in the cattle barn and discovering that some cigarette butts were long enough to find out what it was like to smoke). I mowed the lawn. I was taught to open doors for women—even had to do it for my sister. I was taught to treat women with respect and help them out.

I modeled myself after my dad in some ways but was permitted to change, even subtly encouraged to change how I would be as a man. I was expected to do chores that a generation earlier might have been considered a girl's job. I had to help wash or dry the dinner dishes, taking turns with my sister. I was taught to do some basic cooking.

Over time I began to see changes outside the home and my small community. At the hospital, I noticed men in nurses' garb and women in doctors' garb. My sister went to college, as did most of my female cousins. Although I didn't realize it at the time, a woman going to college was a rather new phenomenon in the '60s.

I witnessed the formation of the women's liberation movement. Although I found some of their demands and demonstrations excessive, the basic message was okay. Women were saying they didn't want to be treated as second-class citizens. I didn't want my sister to be a second-class citizen, so that was fine with me. The drama of the "libbers" may not have been necessary. Or maybe it was.

America's cultural view of gender roles changed due to a lot of factors. Electric devices, such as washing machines, vacuums, and electric mixers, along with the trend toward a smaller family size, meant that women would have more time to expand what they did, including going to work. Some of those jobs meant doing what was historically *men's work*. Rosie the Riveter images certainly gave a push in that direction during World War II, just before I was born. Increased societal pressure to move up in lifestyle made it inevitable that two-income households would be necessary for many families. This led to women nudging increasingly into the work market, even if it was into men's work.

Change often comes hard, and the change in cultural perceptions of gender roles certainly wasn't welcomed by everyone. One poignant incident involving Mom and Dad comes to mind. I'd gotten my driver's license at age sixteen and had been driving a couple years when my sister mentioned that Mom had hinted she wanted to learn to drive. Mom was a rather traditional woman who, some would say, "knew her place," so the fact that her desire to get a driver's license leaked out was significant.

My sister and I, aware that we might be upsetting our dad who we respected and loved, took Mom on the back roads several times to help her practice driving. Mom soon decided she didn't want to get a driver's license. Maybe she didn't like the idea as much as she had anticipated. Maybe she felt guilty about going against Dad's belief. I can only wonder what held her back.

The changes came rather easily for men my age and younger. Many of us embraced the role of being an active dad. I didn't think much about it, I just did it. Looking back, I see irony in how readily I adopted a quite new definition of what it meant to be a male, especially since previously males had it pretty good while dominating America for centuries.

A child learns early in life about pecking orders. I recall thinking as a teenager that men were more important than women. I believe I had that perception because men were the ones who did the physically demanding stuff and generally seemed to be in charge of things. My thinking changed as I grew up. The world was changing. One of my children was a daughter.

Some women want to and can do jobs that our society used to say were men's work. Some men want to and can do jobs that our society used to say were women's work. In some respects this is an indicator that democracy is working—the freedom to choose a work path is a reality embraced by more people. It turns out that my two sons and a daughter each got at least one college degree and moved in traditional career paths. My daughter tabled her chosen career to raise their three children. My sons continue in their chosen careers while being true parenting partners with their spouses. They're comfortable with those choices, so I'm comfortable too.

I feel good about how my children evolved into who they are, but I realize that gender equity is unfinished business in our culture. Issues abound. Equal compensation for equal/similar work. Glass ceilings. Balancing time for self and family. Religions have different views of what gender roles, in the home and in society, should be. Gender roles have been politicized.

When Jake passed my home that day as he spent time with his daughters, he in effect was modeling how some parents today free up each other, so each can experience the freedom to seek and work toward the life they choose. Jake and his wife are also modeling and smoothing the role-shaping road their children will follow as they grow toward adulthood. Time will tell if true gender equity occurs for their children and all children, or if this scene becomes an oddity again.

Q_s

1. What would be different about your life, who you are today, if you had been able to more freely do something as a kid that was the norm for the other gender and not yours?

2. Are there role stereotypes in America for females today? Others for males?

3. Is daily life easier because you can explain your actions as "That's the way men are," or "That's the way women are"? Do you like the dominant stereotypes American culture projects about your gender?

4. What are the pros and cons that describe households with children where both parents work? Who should decide if it's a good, bad, or indifferent thing?

5. America, as with other nations, seems to be transitioning toward acknowledging more than just male and female genders. What is your prediction about how this "Gender Roles" chapter will be rewritten by someone twenty years from now?

Chapter 32

God and Electromagnetic Fields

How do humans and God connect
in day-to-day experiences?

It's difficult, I've discovered, to escape facing *big questions* that come with being a human being. Why am I here? What will happen to me when I die? Is there human-like life beyond our solar system? Is there a supernatural entity throughout space that's the boss? An overarching question for me is "What do I believe, what should I believe about God?" It's important because answers to other questions come better when the supernatural entity question is resolved.

My quest to find answers to these questions has been lifelong. Time blurs memory some, but I am clear in realizing that religion had a major impact on how I began, as a child, to think about life's weighty questions. I grew up in a home in which Christianity was a major guiding force. My childhood answers to major life questions logically mimicked those of my parents. Theirs, in turn, were influenced by views of the Lutheran branch of Christianity. How we "get religion" tends to be a passed on phenomenon.

But children leave the nest. I have been out of the nest a long time. My own set of life experiences and my own thinking continually shape me into the unique person I am. I needed to have my own faith. It wasn't so much that I distrusted the accuracy of answers others had arrived at, as it was a need to find personalized answers that felt real for me.

Developing personal answers to life's big questions doesn't come easily or quickly. It's been like putting together a jigsaw puzzle. As a child I liked doing puzzles on rainy days at our lake cabin. The big picture became clearer one "there it is" at a time. Sometimes I got stuck and looked at the picture on the box cover for help. My quest to solve important puzzles about life has been a similar process—except for the fact I don't have that this-is-what-it'll-look-like picture on a box.

The puzzle pieces that produce a picture of God have come together for me. I am comfortable with where I'm at in understanding how I envision and experience God. My understanding includes much of what I used to believe that fits comfortably with some very different ideas.

It's been a journey. I grew up thinking of God as a very special grandfather type. When I prayed as a child, I imagined myself talking to an elderly man with long graying hair and beard. My image of God then was a combination of awe-inspiring power and human warmth.

A couple religion classes in college broadened my understanding of Christian theology in an academic way. I was introduced to the different ways that people understand God. It wasn't jammed down my throat; we simply were informed and expected to use good critical thinking skills as our faith life grew. I was introduced to new ideas, to mind stretching concepts like realized eschatology and Paul Tillich's concept of God as the ground of being.

My quest has gone beyond academic study. Life experiences complement the scholarly stuff by providing reality checks to what I've been told, what's been passed on to me. I've experienced a lot. As I left the parent-built nest in the mid-sixties, I needed to wonder about society wide dynamics. I couldn't ignore major news events like Sputnik and the Cold War, Vietnam, the Civil Rights Movement, Watergate, and a variety of scandals in government and faith groups. Life events affected how I thought.

Most life experiences are less global in scale, more personal. We interact with other humans. We are a true mix, an often confusing mix. We get along, we fight, we love and care, we act cruelly. I wonder why we act the way we do. Can we get help to be more like who we want to be? Is God involved in the process? How do humans and God interface? Are there supernatural forces that challenge God? If so, are both sides trying to get me on their side?

I wasn't making much progress in explaining God to myself until a drawn out process began—launched by a secular, sci-fi movie. When I first saw *Star Wars* in a theater in 1977, I was intrigued by the movie's concept of The Force. I recognized it as "kinda like what I think about God." The idea went dormant for decades. I can't say what revived it, but The Force analogy resurfaced in 2011.

Crazy as it might seem, the movie helped me better define my personal understanding of God. It made my faith life much more real. The who's and how's and why's tumble into a string of thoughts that answer a lot of my questions about the big questions. My personal understanding of God started to become more real for me.

I was thinking about the *Star Wars* concept of The Force one day when the science of electromagnetic force came to mind. It must have awakened from my high school physics class because it's not a topic I've had much reason to think about. In eleventh grade physics we did experiments and then talked about why bar magnets were either drawn together or pushed away from each other. I heard about magnetic fields. We made a simple generator by putting a coil of copper wire around magnets and adding gears with a shaft and handle. We connected the wire to a basic light fixture, cranked like crazy, and turned on a light bulb. We produced electricity without killing ourselves. We got a gut sense that electricity isn't something we can see, even though it is very real.

I've since learned that energy doesn't just flow through wires; it goes everywhere! Like when as kids we'd slide our feet across a carpet in a low-humidity house, point a finger close to someone else, and both get a shock.

I did a web search in 2012 while drafting this chapter and read that electromagnetism is the interaction responsible for practically all the phenomena encountered in daily life. When Wikipedia contributors added that gravity was the only other force explaining my daily life, I realized I wasn't going to get my head around more than 1 percent of what science geeks (bless 'em) pulled into theirs.

The total web search confirmed for me that God and electromagnetism were somehow connected realities. One of the first thoughts that followed that web search was that electromagnetic phenomena addressed some of the awe and doubt feelings I had when reading parts of the Bible. In theological words, God is omniscient (all knowing) and omnipresent (everywhere). If electromagnetic fields are everywhere then they're also omnipresent. Is God describable, at least in part, as what we humans call electromagnetic force? If so, I have a plausible explanation about how God and I interact! Three puzzle pieces—Star Wars thoughts, electromagnetic force, and thoughts about God—had moved around on my mind's puzzle table in such a way that I received a new understanding about God, very different from my childhood understanding but one that was suddenly very solid.

This new way of thinking, a bold new way for me, needed fleshing out. It's one thing to have a broad concept in mind, another to get it to fit with the nitty grittiness of daily life. I checked out my thinking by regularly examining how it might apply to the variety of aspects that make up day-to-day life. Some of the ways I believe electromagnetic energy, or something like it, helps me understand the way humans interact with God took shape. I'll describe several examples:

1. One example was the relaxation that I felt almost instantly when a friend walked up behind me decades ago and put his hands on my shoulders. He knew from recent conversations how stressed I was when going through a divorce. Did God, through Karl, infuse a comforting "things will work out" feeling in me via electromagnetic conveyance? When I need help of some sort, does God influence the thinking and actions of others through electromagnetic energy in such a manner that they instinctively do something that helps me?

2. When I pray for direction or advice, does God respond through an electromagnetic medium? Is God helping me

control my thinking or actions, especially when I ask for help, by interacting with me through an electromagnetic environment?

3. Sometimes I feel compassion for strangers. When I see people all bundled up biking to work on a Minnesota winter day, I often think a brief prayer, something like, "Give them whatever support they need today." Have I activated a request to God that transforms my compassion into some feeling of renewed energy or hope in a stranger? Could the goals of my prayer then result in them making decisions that improve their day? Did all this happen through some medium, some entity, like electromagnetic energy?

4. I think of my deceased parents sometimes. They are no longer physically here, but is it possible I think of them in certain situations because a memory pops up and guides my thinking and actions? Is it possible they activate memories in me that encourage me or caution me? Do they in some sense still exist and continue expressing love and caring—via God through a phenomenon like the electromagnetic fields?

5. I notice how I now get many *aha* moments as I worship in my church and participate in faith study groups. Does the science of electromagnetic force explain how miracles, like healings, may happen, how waters are calmed, or how Jesus understands people so well?

Christian teachings include references to the Holy Spirit (that, along with God as Father and God as Son (Jesus Christ), form the Trinity concept of God). For years I thought the idea of Holy Spirit was, frankly, kinda weird. Now it makes sense to me. And perhaps more importantly, framing this aspect of God in scientific terms—as electromagnetism being the way that God the Holy Spirit does stuff—results in me consciously interacting much more with God. I understand God better when I consider, what is for me, the probability that God is in part described as either electromagnetism itself or somehow *the one* who manages it better than anyone else.

This chapter has focused on the Christian understanding of God as three parts, the whole. I haven't focused on the Son, Jesus Christ, because, for me, that's the easy part. Central to Christian beliefs is that God sent the history-recorded person we know as Jesus to Earth to help us figure out a whole lot of things, including how to live successfully and happily. I say God the Son is the easy part because Jesus did physically walk with humans for much of his thirty-three years on Earth. The Bible and other documents record things that Jesus said and describes many of the things he did. Most importantly, the fact that the man Jesus died an excruciating death tells me how much God wanted to help us out. That and his teachings and modeling of how to live, how to treat and deal with other humans, is ultimately how I came to believe that God exists. I can't imagine how I would have become a Christian if it weren't for the fact that God chose to become an in-flesh human.

I realize this chapter describes a very non-traditional view of God—very different when I compare it to my childhood view of God. But somewhat surprisingly to me, my newfound understanding of God doesn't negate my earlier understandings. It modifies them, enhances them, and makes them more real. I still think of God as a gray-bearded grandfather sometimes. I still relate to many of the images of God that we talk about in my faith community. Stories in the Bible, if anything, take on deeper meaning. Reading them results in more *aha* insights for me.

I'm now at a point where the puzzle is maybe three-fourths complete. None of us can calculate the percentage done when we don't have a completed picture "on the box cover," and some of the pieces may not have been put on my table yet! But I know I'm more relaxed when life's big questions pop into my mind.

Others may reach a personal understanding of God, through a path somewhat like the one I've described. Maybe electro-magnetic field scientists have made a similar connection. I am curious about what others think, what scientists think, but really don't need to know. Those of us who live life based on a faith that God exists and believe that we humans do fit into planet Earth with a purpose know we can connect to supernatural forces and benefit from that connection. For us, what others think can help. But what others believe can't become my belief, my reality. Each of us must own what we believe.

Thinking of God in the manner posed in this chapter may not work for anyone else. That's okay. It works for me. What I do hope though is that everyone walking a faith life gets to a point, if not already there, that feels real to them and truly helps them get answers to major life questions.

Q_s

1. I got a major puzzle piece to help me put together my picture, my understanding of God, from a sci-fi movie. Sometimes we get help in solving our big questions in surprising ways. What or who helps you to shape your thinking to be more open minded, to consider non-traditional beliefs and ideas?

2. How do you envision God or whatever supernatural entity you relate to?

3. I appreciate the fact that the United States Constitution protects my right to openly be a Christian, including my right to express how I understand God in this chapter. How do you—as a member of a religion or as an atheist or agnostic—rate American Christians in accepting and honoring the rights of others to believe as they do?

Chapter 33

Change Conservatively
and Progressively

**America needs conservative and
progressive thinkers.**

Some of us remember the days when professional home
painters wouldn't touch latex paint. "Oil based paint is the only
paint I'll use" may have been accompanied with some sneering
reference to those who used the new-fangled latex paints.

The professionals said there was a product reason, that oil
based paint was far superior to the latex paints. Many, including some DIYers, agreed when it first hit the market. But there
was also a human nature reason: Latex paint was a new tech-
nology, and many people could not imagine paint performing
well when it was made with water.

Fact is, most of us get cozy comfortable with the known and
many of us are instinctively leery with what is different, new,
not yet experienced.

The oil and latex based products controversy is over. Latex
rules. Oil based paints survive as a niche use. This sea change
in the paint world is now absorbed into our culture. I say good
for the latex paint pioneers, and thanks to the oil holdouts that

kept the criticism pressure on the latex people until they had a darn good product.

I can't imagine any change being totally positive. I found out, for example, that it's much better to use oil based varnish for indoor wood window frames. Frost buildup in the winter time lifted the latex varnish where the wood and glass meet on the bottom edge of my kitchen's energy efficient windows.

Despite the imperfections that accompany changes, change is a fact of life for us as individuals, from paint decisions to much weightier issues. Change is a constant beyond our personal lives. It happens in virtually any facet of American life. In many respects *change* is the primary dynamic with which a society must grapple in order to govern itself well.

The reality of change creates a dilemma for Americans. Since *managing* change is central to the success of America, it follows that we need to have an effective mechanism to get good change management to happen. We are a highly politicized nation, so the first finger quite accurately points directly at the political system we have—and that means we have a problem.

> *WARNING!! Today's politicians think "party and personal survival." They don't problem solve intelligently. We have to reshape them.*

The rhetoric coming out of the mouths of politicians and their party leadership doesn't look at the pros and cons of change dynamics. Politician rhetoric comes from people more interested in rousing emotion-driven support than dealing with every day, nitty-gritty issues like managing the specific change dynamics coming at us. When observing politicians in action, it becomes apparent that thoughtful dialog and the hard work of gathering solid, unbiased information are not excitement arousing enough to attract the interest of the party faithful and the financial supporters. (That statement is too kind—it's really that parties have become too partisan to be willing to gather solid, unbiased information.)

What about those of us who want our nation to consider each change that appears—each on its own merit—through a process that roots out the pros and cons. Brainstorming by thoughtful and reasonably informed people; checking out the work of good, unbiased scientist types; and then deciding what to do needs to be our change management process. *And then* we can decide to stop or resist a change, or support it, but manage it in an ongoing way.

The political situation in the early twenty-first century is a pretty bleak landscape. Party politicians generally are unabashedly biased, partisan, and not the problem solving and future strategizing persons we need. Maybe it's time to join those Americans among us who already ignore political parties in our country. It's time more of us work to reshape how our elected leaders think and behave.

Instead of going with partisan politicians let's simply go for leaders, in every aspect of American society, to think about change as progressive leaning and conservative leaning. Please don't think of progressives as Democrats and conservatives as Republicans. That terminology, as thrown about by politicians and the media, is simply another politician-concocted smoke screen to confuse us, to distract us.

What we need is to demand simple, clear definitions: A progressive action is one that promotes a change. A conservative action is one that resists a change.

Of course no one promotes every change that comes along. Even those who are naturally comfortable with the idea of change will at times resist, even deplore, some changes. Likewise no one resists every change that comes along. Even those who regularly react negatively to change and usually resist change will gradually accept, even welcome some changes. We all have our leanings based on our personality and life experiences. America needs leaners toward change and leaners that resist change. The fact we have both is very good for America.

Party labels don't mean much to me anymore. They are a distraction that I work to ignore. I wish they'd go away. Rather than sit back and accept the political shenanigans we currently suffer through, we would be better off personally ignoring party lines, cherry pick candidates (including independents), and only re-elect the precious few current office holders who ground their speaking and their voting on very defendable information. I think we'll discover that we instinctively will choose some change leaners and some change resisters.

> *We shape elected representatives by how we talk about them (the word gets around) and how we personally interact with them.*

How do we shape elected representatives? Through a variety of actions. We stop writing checks to any political party and start writing checks to highly-qualified, good-thinking candidates who demonstrate time-honored values. We need individuals who dare to genuinely think and act on behalf of all Americans, not as puppets for a political party or big financial contributors. We contact them, visit their town hall meetings, and let them know we want them to put America ahead of partisan, selfish interests as programmed by a political party and those with money and other forms of out-of-balance power. By doing such things we begin to shape their thinking away from party politics toward true problem solving and wise strategic planning.

Political parties as we now suffer through them seem to be here to stay. We as individuals need to step up to the plate. America needs individuals who speak up with cautionary voices so that we don't willy-nilly let go of customs, values, viewpoints, strategies, and products that have served us well. And we need people to push the envelope and help America respond to and shape the always changing future.

We need change leaners and change resisters who are willing to dialog. We need people to examine change that has started or been suggested, to think through the change, understand what outcomes it will produce. What positives? What negatives? We need to prepare ourselves to watch for unintended consequences and figure out how to respond if/ when they happen.

How great would it be if Congress and other legislative bodies were willing to engage in civil dialog, even tug-o-wars, to look at the pros and cons of promoting a change. I think they'd sleep well at night and feel better about themselves if they did.

We can help them do that. Maybe, if we remind them about how we changed paint types, noting the ups and downs that occurred as we transitioned from oil dominance to latex dominance, we could help them understand the concept of wisely considering change that affects our culture in more comprehensive ways.

Q*s*

1. How do you respond to changes that come at you?

2. What are some changes you have adopted, or simply resigned yourself to accept? Have you dug in your heels against some of them and then later embraced and appreciated the change?

3. What are some changes you have made but later regretted?

4. Will America fall apart or be better off if we shuck party politics? Is the rather large number of Americans who don't affiliate with a political party a factor in your thinking?

Chapter 34

When Religion and Politics Unite

**What happens when the passion of faith beliefs
links up with the passion of politics?**

A few decades ago a change in America's political scene drew my attention. The Republican Party (GOP), which was moving further to the conservative right, and *leaders* of some of the "Christian Right" were collaborating—promoting similar agendas, meeting together. This phenomenon made me feel uneasy. This discomfort level increased in recent years and, as we watched the 2016 presidential election cycle play out, alarmed me.

All political parties have always worked to attract large blocks of voters to join them. Getting more followers translates into more votes, and getting elected to run America's governments is what political parties are all about. However, in my observation it's unusual to have two organizations with quite different mission statements join forces. The fact that this phenomenon has nationwide impact means we need to make very sure we study it well.

I get that the Christian Right and the GOP would see advantages to joining forces. Political parties formed (to the chagrin of several of our nation's founders) shortly after America's government was first set up. They formed to recruit supporters for opposing views of how America's government should be run. Religions, on the other hand, formed so that followers of a specific faith leader (Jesus for example) could better help each other understand their beliefs and support each other in living the lifestyle their religious beliefs promoted.

It seems to me that when two such differently purposed groups in effect merge, one or both is contaminating and infecting its mission. That seems to be clearly the case for the conservative Christian religion. How can Christianity stay true to the teachings and modeling of Christ while getting mixed up in rancorous and polarizing politics? The Christian message is being infected by actions that are counter to the teachings of Christ. At the very least, Christian messages about how to treat other people, including those who disagree with you and those who are down and out, seem to be disregarded. What image of Christianity are people observing? Will some seekers drop any thoughts of attending and joining Christian congregations because they see hypocrisy or see behaviors to which they don't want to be linked?

This book makes the point that our values and points of view are shaped by many influences, and those are the values we give to our kids. I will describe some influences that I believe shaped what I'm putting on America's discussion table in this chapter.

When I first sensed this collaboration occurring over a decade ago, I simply tried to understand what was going on. I wanted to know why it was discomforting to me. I had not noticed religion and politics working together in such a public manner during the first forty to fifty years of my life. In this book I've opened myself up to readers by describing how my faith life has gotten to where it is today. But I haven't described my involvement with political parties much other than describing my growing, personal distaste for them.

I grew up in Republican country and was pretty involved in party activity starting in the mid-1950s. I joined the Teenage Republican Club in my home town and still have campaign buttons from that era. I was a teenage page at the Republican state convention and was fairly active with Young Republicans in college. I drifted away from most political party activity but continued participating in election year party caucus meetings; I wanted to have input into America's future. The Democrats were overwhelmingly dominant in NE Minnesota where the first thirty years of my career were lived. I attended their caucuses in large part because it was through them that I could have the most impact. In addition I saw their issue positions addressing needs I observed in some of my students and their families.

> *Denomination: a religious organization whose congregations are united in their adherence to its beliefs and practices.*
> *(Merriam-Webster Dictionary)*

There was no clue during all that activity that a segment of Christianity would someday work so closely with a political party. It seemed to my teenage level of experience that separation of church and state was taken literally. I understood the separation to mean it was important for a religious person to be involved in the political process—but only as individuals and not as a denomination in a religion.

There's been dramatic change. Some ministers in some Christian churches are openly active in politics. The issue positions of these church leaders and those of the increasingly strident right wing of the GOP became strikingly similar on various topics—the planet's environment, international relations, and social issues such as abortion, gay marriage, terrorism, and immigration.

We're now seeing a significant portion of the "planks" of one party's platform lining up with some denominational position statements on societal issues. In fact, leaders of some conservative Christian groups very publicly grill candidates to make sure they're going to support theological positions. Some right wing Christian denomination leaders are openly endorsing candidates. Some Christian church leaders now serve as spokespersons for Republican candidates. All of that used to be taboo within Christianity.

> *Strife synonyms: trouble, conflict, discord, contention, fighting, dissention, friction, rivalry.*
>
> *(Merriam-Webster Dictionary)*

I am concerned for my nation. I am concerned for Christianity, my personal faith choice. America is in the most partisan and polarized period of time that I've observed in the fifty years since I could first vote. Christianity doesn't need, no religion needs, more reasons to argue, and the politically polarized state of America today automatically means religion + politics = strife.

There is no one Christian position on political issues. There is no single spokesperson or single official group for Christianity in America. Simply implying that a congregation or one denomination of Christianity can speak for all of Christianity in the political scene is in itself divisive. The way individual Christians and particular denominations understand Christianity is certainly their own choice and right. I say so as someone who supports the first amendment's freedom of speech and freedom of religion; they *are* rights. I also say so as a Christian who sees some of the theological and specific issue positions of the Christian Right as different from my views, while yet seeing unity on many other positions.

The reality is that some Christians understand the Bible and the teachings and modeling of Jesus as recorded during his thirty-three years on Earth quite differently. As a result, not all Christian individuals or groups agree on policies and actions about war, wealth distribution, the environment, social programs, rights of individuals vs the rights of community, and views toward peoples of other nations.

We individuals who are actively engaged in *any* religion need to be very thoughtful before deciding how to best exercise our rights and responsibilities to help shape America's future by joining and leveraging our impact through *any* political party. I choose to promote my understanding of Christianity as an individual and through my church community instead of pushing any political party to do that for me.

Q*s*

1. If you are a follower of a religion, how do you express your faith in the political arena?

2. How might Christians, non-Christians, atheists, or agnostics respond or react differently to this chapter?

3. Do you believe it's constitutionally okay for a Christian denomination to closely collaborate with a political party? What about Buddhists, Hindus, Muslims, Unitarians, and other religious groups?

Chapter 35

Wife Caught Me Red-Handed

**The dynamics of getting along
with someone takes skill and compromise.**

I was working at the kitchen table one day when I heard a car door's muffled slam. Moments later the breezeway door latch clicked. No knock, no doorbell. I knew it had to be my wife.

I panicked, a sick-in-the-stomach kind of panic.

I am semi-retired and have a home office in the basement. It's dreary down there. I also like variety, so I work in different parts of the house. But the fact that I'm a multi-tasker of sorts is what really explains why I instinctively panicked. On that day I happened to have four projects going in four locations in the house. My wife hates clutter and sees four projects scattered around her neat home as clutter. Didn't matter that they were *productive piles*, didn't matter that they were *rather neat piles*.

I stammered something like, "What brings you home at 12:30 on a work day?" Sandy later told me that the look on my face was hysterical.

I survived. Our marriage survives.

Sandy and I married in 1995, second marriages for both of us. A work friend made an interesting comment to me after I told her I was getting married to Sandy. Speaking from personal experience, she said "It'll go well; you work harder in a second marriage." Sandy and I do work hard in this second marriage at making our relationship succeed.

The work is sometimes easy, sometimes an effort. I try to reduce my tendency to clutter to accommodate her tendency toward neatness. It's one of my keep-our-relationship-healthy efforts. (Sandy has her own list.) Our home is grand central for our daily lives. Determining how neat the place should look is simply one specific, one dynamic in our complex relationship. The piles = clutter = strain on relationship dynamic happens to be a biggy for us. It's not something to be ignored. When ignored I can literally feel an anchor is putting a drag on a positive, fulfilling, happy marriage.

Any two people are players in the dynamics that affect how their relationship goes. Some dynamics drag the relationship into negative feelings and results. Some lift the relationship into the "I like being around you; I like doing things with you" level. The overall success of a relationship depends on how well we nurture the positives and how well we deal with the clutter-piles issues that strain feelings.

People in any type of relationship need to continually work on plans to modify or otherwise resolve relationship anchor drags. That's pretty hard to achieve without doing some compromising. Fortunately, noticing the rewards of working out a wise compromise bolsters the willingness to continue efforts to make relationships work.

The dynamics of getting along with someone, accomplishing what good relationships do through collaboration, takes skill. When people in a marriage relationship learn those skills, they benefit and America benefits. Our culture, our nation benefits because relationship problem-solving and collaboration skills naturally follow us wherever we go. Goodness knows, America could use more of us getting along with people we live with, work with, and interact with during our daily activity.

I've learned a lot about how relationships move in positive and negative directions through observation and working on skill building. Marriage has given me a comprehensive, 24/7/365 opportunity to try different ways to talk about our different habits, different quirks, different values, and the host of other issues that affect how we interact.

We have choices as we talk. The continuum runs from unproductive arguing and other actions that sour our relationship to consciously moving in a productive direction. Modifying who we are, yet maintaining our core, as we work out a compromise. Sometimes we need to get a third party perspective. Skillful counsellors can be very helpful when we as clients are honest with ourselves, want the relationship to be better, and are willing to do some hard work.

The work required to make America more harmonious and productive—from social clubs to cities to our humongous nation—is more difficult and complex because of the sheer numbers and generally much less personal nature of relationships. But doing this hard work is critically important to keep our various communities healthy.

Fortunately, the tasks involved and skills required in this work are similar whether in a marriage-type relationship or in the workplace, neighborhoods, organizations, and governing bodies. Work at communicating and identifying problems before they get out of hand. Cut each other some slack about contrasting views, habits, and lifestyles. Make good faith efforts to accommodate each other, giving compromise a chance.

As with a marriage, governing a nation requires that individuals realize that in a democracy they can't always "win" or "be right." A democracy requires a sharing of power, finding solutions that promote win–win. If these values do not operate in a marriage, the marriage fails. The union is dissolved. The risks are the same for our nation. Americans need to do the work that makes personal relationships function well. When we do, we helpfully model, perhaps inspire, other Americans to do the same. When we do such things we do our part to help America become more harmonious and productive.

Life threw me a marriage curve during lunch time that day. Curves happen in all settings of life. Developing good relationship-producing and maintaining skills means we will be better prepared and less prone to feelings of panic.

Q_s

1. Do Americans spend enough time and energy on building and maintaining relationships? What alerts you to a need to spend more effort on a family, friend, work, or neighbor relationship?

2. What values in our American culture become stronger when we devote time and effort to make a relationship better?

3. What strategy works well for you when you decide it's time to speak to a spouse or friend about a problem you perceive in the relationship?

Addendum: Sandy and I divorced three years after I wrote this chapter. We decided, with the help of many hours of counselling and lots of in-depth conversation that we are better "Good Friends Forever" than spouses. There was never any shouting or meanness. There were no blame games in explaining to ourselves how such early married happiness came to this. We shared an attorney to do the paperwork. We talk on the phone regularly and still do dinner and other stuff together once in a while. What once was a conceptual goal (to be GFFs) has become a gut feel and a naturally expressed good relationship.

It's understandable that readers will say I'm a hypocrite, that I don't practice what I preach. Guilty. I've missed the mark not only about making two marriage relationships work but also about other themes promoted in this book. Please realize that all of my mistakes in life have given me opportunities to learn and to grow and I've generally felt I've moved on wiser. I wish for readers the strength and support needed to learn and grow should the mark be missed in personal aims, whether it is a commitment to a spouse or any other goal.

Divorce sucks. It's not what I want to model to my kids and grandchildren. Sandy and I are recovering. My first divorce was my biggest disappointment in myself, so you can imagine how I feel about divorcing a second time. Its small consolation but I feel good that we are at least modeling how a marriage can dissolve in a very civil way. I love Sandy as a great friend, a good feeling that fuels GFF.

Chapter 36

Leadership in America

**America's future lies in the hands
of its leaders and its followers.**

As a parent, teacher, and now grandparent I've had frequent opportunities to observe how young humans interact. One fascinating dynamic is how some emerge as leaders and some as followers. One puzzle I was driven to solve as a junior high teacher was why one class of students was so different from another. Same subject matter, same room, same age group, same teacher—yet very different atmospheres. I needed to figure out how some of my five classes per day were so productive and easy to relate to while others challenged my classroom management skills.

I think I figured it out. I believe one or two kids in a neighborhood somehow morph into leadership roles very early in life. They're not elected, don't consciously seek the role, but somehow it happens. Perhaps it's one kid who becomes popular as a goofball and others follow. Or maybe the young minds are drawn to someone who is really kind and helpful, or athletic, or smart, or cute.

Neighborhood groups merge when they start grade school and the "voting process" starts again. Kids naturally are drawn to certain kids. The conscious and subconscious reasons probably change as we get older, but at some point some people get the feeling they're seen as leaders and others get the feeling they're followers.

This emerging leadership process can get messy. I've watched as secondary school student leaders spar, usually more psychological warfare than anything else. As students grow older, the desire to be the leader becomes more conscious and strategically orchestrated by those who've survived the leadership quest through the winnowing process of middle school.

By adulthood, becoming a leader becomes very serious business for those who have found a leadership niche that they want to keep. They consciously seek the influence, the power, the adulation, and often the financial benefits that go with being a leader.

> *Altruism: feelings and behavior that show a desire to help other people and a lack of selfishness*
>
> *(Merriam-Webster Dictionary)*

What this means for a society is incredibly significant for a couple reasons. A lot of leadership skills have been shaped, and the experience in leading projects and people can be invaluable. The other reason is that by now fully emerged leaders have taken a fork in the road: some leader-strivers do so for personal gain and others do so for altruistic motives. Feeling power and liking the accompanying lofty status goes to the head for many. But, fortunately, not all. There are many examples of leaders who lead humble lives, sacrifice personal time or wealth, and come across as being more others-oriented than self-oriented. I think we all personally know more than one of the wonderfully "average," unsung heroes and heroines who live in our neighborhoods.

Leaders matter. How they lead really matters, really affects how a nation and its culture develop. Three American institutions are positioned to influence, to lead America into its future: government, businesses and faith communities. In what direction are leaders in charge of these three areas taking us today? Here are some general observations.

Government. The role of government is to run our nation, to problem solve and strategize a thoughtful, wise future. Elected officials on the national and state levels of government are currently too prone to be mired in the quagmire of partisan bickering and personal power acquisition to be called altruistic leaders. Many people in elected positions are dragging America down.

The American people need better, our kids deserve better. We desperately need positive leadership, successful negotiators, and skilled problem solvers in our government who will stop fueling the bickering and choose to govern in a civil manner.

Business. From the people's viewpoint, the role of business is to produce useful products or provide needed services, create jobs for those able to work, and of course make a profit. To what extent should we expect a degree of altruistic leadership from the business community? They benefit by operating in the United States. They benefit from a system of roads and other infrastructure; they benefit from law enforcement that permits them to focus on their business. A portion of them get some form of financial or other government assistance. And Americans provide a huge consumer base that on average is financially positioned to buy their products and services. Businesses get benefits from us. Do their leadership teams discuss how they can and should "give back" to America? Do they give back?

I am personally aware of and thank those businesses, of all sizes and types, that genuinely include in their business model statements that, in effect, say "we will help our nation and help provide for the general wellbeing of the American people". We are blessed with some truly admirable, relatively selfless—and profitable—business leaders. America's business leaders have overall done many things to make the United States a powerful nation. I hope more and more are seeking to, for example, share the benefits of a recovering economy with the American people through more hiring and better wages. Those would be altruistic actions.

Faith Communities. Faith communities by whatever name generally do promote altruistic attitudes and behaviors. Their leadership role in communities of any size is essentially built into a central reason for their existence. Good leadership results when the faithful start living out the noble goals of doing good things for other people. Leadership in making Golden Rule communities often results in a ripple effect due to a premise common across faith groups: when a person helps others without expecting something in return the action is appreciated and returned—the serving others concept spreads and faith group membership often grows.

Leadership in this sector of American society, however, has two weak spots. One is that the leaders are dispersed, often not collaborative, and sometimes competitive. Faith leaders are certainly not immune from having power/adulation go to their heads to the point that altruistic behaviors become secondary. This dynamic can occur as leaders get together within a religion or across religions. Nonetheless, faith leaders on average provide excellent, sometimes courageous, leadership for America.

Another damper on good leadership from faith communities is that the percentage of Americans who are active members has declined. The reality is that even truly good leaders may have fewer followers, and their collective impact on the quality of life in America is diminished.

Wherever leaders come from, there have to be followers. Leaders by definition can't lead without followers, and followers are often aimless and can flounder without a leader.

Where is America at with our followers, in other words, most of us? It seems counterintuitive, but the reality is that the masses of people in our democracy and economic system drive leaders. We have power. Leaders can't lead without our support. We have opportunities to vote, to pressure our elective government leaders. We have buying power that makes or breaks businesses. Religious leaders have checks on their power, their success level.

America's future lies in our hands, whether we're in structured, formal leadership positions or acting as engaged, responsible followers. The individuals who rise above the pettiness (of which we're now seeing too much) are looked up to as setting a standard we wish all leaders and followers could achieve. Such individuals step in to redirect those who are unproductively arguing or throwing insults back-and-forth. They help those who bicker figure out how to listen better, compromise, and work out their differences. Such leaders and followers help reduce tensions, put a lid on emotional outbursts, and smooth out and repair relationships.

People on the street know that the quality of leadership in the United States has declined dramatically. A senior citizen I talked with while campaigning door-to-door in 2010 brought up the topic when I asked if there was anything in particular he wanted me to work for if elected. He said "We need statesmen in government, not what we have now." I was pleased to hear this retiree use the term, *statesmen,* and I got his point. The dictionary definition that fits the way I heard this man use it is "a wise, skillful, and respected political leader." Enough said?

America needs good leadership in government, business, and faith communities. America needs leadership that places the best interests of the whole nation above the interests of a few. We need more statesmen, more stateswomen, to wisely lead America. We'll get them as we plant the altruistic seed in our children and see what happens when leaders and followers demonstrate feelings and behaviors that show a desire to help other people and a lack of selfishness.

Q_s

1. In what ways can American leaders do better?

2. It can be said that discussing leadership in only three categories is too limiting. How would you broaden the discussion?

3. Jobs have been off-shored; people are hired to find loopholes in tax laws; headquarters are shifted to other countries so as to pay a foreign country's lower taxes instead of paying taxes to support America. Who is responsible to lead America to resolve the issues of business rights and the rights of Americans who are hurt by the business actions mentioned? What might good compromises look like?

4. Is their a down side to stressing altruism as the guiding principle for good leadership?

Chapter 37

Here's Proof!

**People in a democracy must seek
truly good information.**

It was probably in my junior high years that I watched a shaving commercial on TV that is still a vivid memory. An award winning ad? Not! It was a phony pitch, one easily seen as such even by a young teenager.

Verbally extolling the virtues of this brand of shaving cream, a voiceover seductively announced, "Here's proof!" The screen shifted to an *animated* drawing of a man's stubbly cheek, enlarged to show detail. The animation showed the beard smothered with white foam (using five times the amount needed). An animated shaver blade swooped across the face and the beard hairs were cut off. At skin level. Completely. In one swipe.

The "proof" shown, the screen switched back to a can of the shaving cream, so that we would recognize it on a store shelf and go right to it, ignoring inferior competitor brands.

I remember thinking to myself, "an animation is proof?" Of course it wasn't proof. Proof that the shaving cream worked better than any other would require carefully designed and conducted lab research, the kind that *Big Bang Theory* minds do. I vowed to never use the product when I was old enough to shave!

What causes beard hair to stand up so the blade cuts it instead of sliding over it? For that matter, does shaving cream cause hair to stand up? I'm not a facial hair expert and not a shaving cream scientist that could offer testable answers to such questions. I do know, however, that an animated description of shaving does nothing to prove anything about shaving. Getting proof, providing proof, takes work. It requires analytical and critical thinking. It requires an open mind. It takes a driven mind, one that considers options to what is heard, read, or looked up in only one source.

The level of importance in getting proof is very different for shaving cream and weightier matters. Determining if we can trust advertisements and commercials affects us as individuals. If we've worked to get a good education, have a good mind, and use it well, we have no one to blame other than ourselves when we buy a shabby product based on a sell-job that caught us napping.

News sources and politicians significantly ramp up the need to check for proof, to be convinced. These two sources are for most people the most common way that information is obtained about how America is doing, what government is doing, and what direction we should be taking. Unfortunately too many politicians intentionally give us incomplete information, don't mention that actual facts only fit a certain context. Sometimes they and media flat-out make statements that aren't true. Such scamps unethically only want support for their agenda so supplying verifiable proof is avoided instead of provided.

People in a democracy need, must have, good information to wisely guide and participate in governance, to weigh in on problem solving and how to shape the nation's future. Unfortunately, there are boulders strewn on the road we need to negotiate to get good information, the proof we need.

Some political organizations (parties, special interest groups, PACs) suffer from "thought incest." Leaders and followers impregnate each other with what evolves into group think, a narrow and biased interpretation of reality. Such dynamics often spawn emotional, highly energized rejection of good information and views resulting in incestuous group think. Share bad information often enough and some people actually seem to believe it instead of what honest fact and proof gathering would reveal.

Our nation is sometimes blindsided as outcomes of incestuous group think decisions are discovered to have ignored facts and perspectives that could have led to wiser decisions and better outcomes. Better decisions weren't considered because they didn't fit the ideology of the Democratic or Republican parties or other special interest groups.

It is way too simple to only criticize the currently dysfunctional political party scene. The impulse to believe what we want to believe and to hang out with people who think as we do resides in all of us. We accept assertions with flimsy proof, if any proof at all. We are impressed by facts, figures, and quotes and decide "somebody looked into this so I don't need to, how nice that I get the benefit of their hard work." How glibly and foolishly we are sucked into believing rubbish information when we follow the easy route.

Government leaders and we the people can't follow the easy

route. We all must train ourselves to be skeptical, to demand worthy proof so we aren't duped by phony shaving commercials, partisan politicians, and other hucksters.

Q*s*

1. How do you feel when you've been hoodwinked, taken advantage of, duped, or whatever you call it?

2. It's human nature to like people who think like we do. Perhaps we see it as an endorsement of our good thinking! What makes understanding and managing this natural impulse so difficult?

3. How do we push businesses and political campaigns to provide verifiable support for what they sell and declare?

Chapter 38

At the Bus Stop

We need each other.

I noticed a couple at a bus stop on 86th Street one windy, cold January morning. At first I saw their shapes in silhouette—a large, nearly round person and a slim, taller person. They were side by side, facing my way as they watched for their bus.

As my pickup brought me closer, I saw them in more detail. The heavy-set person was an adult woman in an open jacket, unbuttoned perhaps because it didn't fit her large frame well. The tall man wore a cap and what looked like a warmer coat. They were close together, and in passing I saw that each had an arm around the other.

The image captivated me. What made two seemingly ordinary people standing at a bus stop so striking? Where do people go on a bus early on a Saturday morning, especially on a brutally cold day? Did they have jobs? What was there relationship to each other? What were their circumstances? Was the woman's coat a hand-me-down?

All this wondering, I realized, was off track. All I could do was guess at answers. Yes, it would have been nice to get to know more about them, to find out who they were, to know why they were at that bus stop on a cold, windy day. It would have been nice to know answers to all of my questions. But the questions that came to mind weren't the source of my being so taken when seeing them. It was something I sensed in the few seconds they came into view as I drove toward them.

I understood finally that it was the image itself, like the *Mona Lisa* or that farm couple with a pitch fork in *American Gothic*. Some images just grab our attention, make us pause to study, to imagine, and ultimately to feel somehow enriched by the simple mental exercise of wondering what's going on.

It's worth paying attention to what piques our interest. Life can be enriched, I have discovered, from what flows out of curiosity, inspiration, and empathy.

The non-verbal message that struck me that morning is something that I still think about, wonder about. The image etched so powerfully that I can pull it up from my memory drive to study it and try to figure it out. That bus stop image has become my Mona Lisa.

I believe it is their standing together—close, side by side— that captures my attention. It was how they had an arm around each other. It was the look from their faces that I caught in those few seconds. Their gazes were steady, not animated and neither joyful nor sad. Two people waiting for a bus. Together. In a simple embrace.

My sense of the "bus stop couple" is that they probably didn't have much in the material sense. But they had each other. When I've seen people put an arm around someone as this couple did, it usually is done as an expression of caring. A need to give comfort, a need to receive it. An action that says so much more than words. Maybe their arms moved to a simple embrace because of their particular purpose in taking a bus that day, such as visiting a friend who was hospitalized.

As I recall that scene now, I am reminded of important life lessons. We need more than food, clothing, and shelter to lead full, happy lives. We need people who care about us. We need people who will put their arms around us, for big reasons or no reason at all. We need such "things" more than we realize. Gourmet food, top-shelf clothing, and palatial homes don't fill the need. Luxury cars and decked out 4x4s, all-inclusive vacations, and monster sized TVs don't fill the need.

My guess is that the couple at the bus stop didn't have a lot of material things, but I am convinced that they had something the majority of us don't appreciate enough, don't give and receive often enough. They had each other. They benefit from that gut feeling, a reality more often felt than thought about, that binds humans together and fills out a sense of being human in a very deep way. Touches. Someone to confide in. Relax with. Talk to. Rely on. Cry with. Laugh with. Enjoy doing things with.

Have we lost our way in twenty-first century America? Have we extolled materialism to the point that we are less human, less truly connected to other human beings? Has greed and materialism given us a false sense of what being happy and successful really means?

Q_s

1. Have you captured similar mental photo's that stick with you, cause you to reflect? If so, what are they, and what kind of thinking or feelings do they produce in you?

2. What stories of your life experiences stand out for you because they help you understand what really is important in life? Do you strive to remember and use these understandings?

3. Are you ever surprised to realize you find profound value in lessons that somehow are transmitted from persons you perceived to be rather different than you?

Chapter 39

America's Health

**I felt the pulse of America's people—
and it was good.**

I experienced the Mayo Clinic in Rochester, Minnesota, for the first time in November of 2014. The clinic is of course a well-known and respected source of health care. But it was something beyond Mayo's formal purpose that led me to a valuable insight. I got a sense of how healthy our nation is during the half day I was there.

I felt the pulse of America's people and it was good.

The atrium at the Rochester campus of Mayo Clinic greeted me soon after entering the Gonda building. The atrium is spacious and uplifting in its architecture. Its ceiling reaches up about thirty feet, and the exterior wall, almost all glass, brightened up the area even on that dreary November day. A grand piano and a wide, curving stairway down from the check-in level gives the area the feel of a grand ballroom.

The first people image that focused my attention on the activity in this area of the clinic came from a glance at a twenty-something woman in a wheelchair as we passed each other. I wondered why such a young woman would be coming to

Mayo, a place where some people come because they have an unusual need. A young man—husband, boyfriend, or simply a good friend—was with her. There are times in our lives, it occurred to me, when we really need someone at our side, and she had that someone.

Seconds later I saw an elderly man shuffling slowly with the aid of a four-footed cane. A woman about the same age walked beside him. Her voice was soft. The upward pitch endings of the comments I partially heard suggested she was an encouraging, supportive person—friend, wife, or both. The look on the man's face implied resolve, but a resolve modified with a touch of "whatever will be, will be—que sera, sera." Whatever he found out that day, whatever would be his future, would be heard and somehow shared with someone at his side.

Later, as I passed through the atrium to get to the cafeteria, I saw three women approaching in silky flowing clothing that revealed only their eyes and hands. I pondered how rapidly the American culture seems to absorb people from other cultures. Some Americans gin up animosity as they stereotype all who wear "clothes like this" as terrorists. I didn't sense that here. Not even curious stares.

That impressed me. Americans generally are gracious in continuing the tradition of welcoming and becoming interactive with the ongoing waves of people who come to America to seek better lives. I know enough about my ancestors coming to the U.S. to know that they appreciated the welcoming attitudes they experienced. Perhaps other people at Mayo that day reflected as I did on the fact that we were immigrants once too. Perhaps people who need this clinic have more of a sense that we're all in the same needing-help boat.

Settling in at a cafeteria table for a late breakfast, I noticed a forty-something woman several tables away who was sitting across from an older woman with her back to me. The younger woman's face was almost expressionless. I glanced at her periodically to see what her next look might be, but it didn't change. Was it sadness? Boredom? Resigned and muted anguish?

My curiosity piqued, I made sure my sweeping gazes around the room included a look at her. Perhaps the sixth time I glanced at her, I was almost startled. Her face was transformed 100 percent—it was radiant! I couldn't hear her voice but her face said she was speaking from a light and energized feeling. I noticed an elderly man in a volunteer vest walking away; he turned around and walked back to the table. He talked to "radiant face," and it dawned on me that this volunteer must have somehow produced the transformation I'd seen in this woman.

I guessed that moments earlier he had seen the same noticeable face I had and pulled a trick out of his bag that had a very positive impact on the woman's mood. It probably was a simple comment that conveyed caring and interest in a lighthearted way that infused the look of happiness that I needed to wait to see. An elderly volunteer, likely a total stranger, turned this woman's day around, into a more positive experience. What a gift he bestowed, at no charge, with no expectation that he would get more than a good feeling in return.

My series of appointments that day meant I passed through the atrium several times. As I walked in one of the hallways that connected to it, I heard an absolutely beautiful soprano voice. The volume increased as I approached the atrium where

I saw a slender girl standing by the grand piano next to a somewhat older woman accompanying her on the piano. People were standing quietly along the second floor railing, on the grand entrance stairway, and near the musicians.

We were transfixed. Uplifted. Distracted. Unburdened. This young woman couldn't have expected to know the group of people she helped out. But she must have known that people who needed to be uplifted, distracted, and unburdened would appreciate her presence and gift of music. I found out later that some people regularly put "sing at Mayo's grand piano" on their calendars. Some Americans go out of their way to give the gift of time in a way that lifts up people who are down.

Other people images stimulated my senses throughout the day. Not the least was the caring attitude of so many who came to the clinic to earn a paycheck. I suppose a few were good actors, company policy and supervisory guidelines and admonitions making them so. But I got the definite feeling from those with whom I interacted that they put on their health care roles each work day because they truly wanted to help people who needed help.

Clinic hours were over when I headed toward the parking ramp. My doctor didn't prescribe it, but I bought a Dairy Queen malt in the underground shopping center anyway. I chose to sit and finish it near the elevator before heading to my car. I'd picked up many *people messages* during my day at Mayo, and wanted to collect my thoughts to better understand how I felt about what I'd seen.

My take-away from my observations that November day is that the vital signs of the American people are very good. When the chips are down, when individuals are going through tough times, Americans step up to do what's right, what's good, what's needed to make this a nation that takes care of those who need it; a nation that steps up to the plate when things need to get done.

The process of how individuals make decisions to help out those who are struggling is sometimes a simple, instinctive response. The phrase "my heart went out to them" reflects that. A very high percentage of people get those feelings, even people many stereotype as gruff, rough and uncaring. Seeing pain in a person's face can open a good person's heart. Seeing a young child who needs very intensive care can do that. Seeing the accompanying parent or grandparent whose time and daily schedule has only rare stretches of free time can do that.

Thoughts on my ninety-minute drive back to Bloomington gave me a good feeling. I'd observed many examples of Americans helping people in need. We celebrate that fact, and we publicly honor those who do so during events like the 9-11's, Katrina's, and Sandy Hook's of our world. It is a pleasure to see that local news media have moved in a direction of seeking out examples from the daily stories of people just doing the right thing whenever and wherever situations beg for such good neighbor action.

Perhaps even more Americans will collectively make such stepping up a daily habit. Perhaps we'll learn to step up regardless of who is in need, regardless of cultural differences, regardless of personality differences. Helping others in need creates a good feeling, and feeling good is a part of personal wellbeing, a neat impetus to do more to contribute to America's good health.

Q_s

1. In your experience, what impresses you about the generous, helpful nature of people you know?
2. Are their times when it is legitimate, even appropriate, to not be generous? Are there some situations when truly trying to be helpful is tricky or risky?
3. What bogus reasons are given by some to "explain" why they aren't generous or helpful?

Chapter 40

Sunshine

**Our values determine what legacy
we pass on to our kids.**

Granddaughter Kate's favorite song for many weeks was "Tomorrow" from the children's version of the musical *Annie* that she had recently seen. She was singing it as I walked into her home one day. Kate has a good singing voice but my smile was prompted even more by the contented happiness I saw on her face. (I saw the same Stages Theater production in July 2016 with Sandy and a grandniece. I walked out not only singing several *Annie* songs but feeling generally upbeat.)

"Tomorrow" starts out with a phrase that popped into my head as I thought about what I wanted to communicate in this concluding chapter. The sun will come out tomorrow sums up the way I feel as I look into our grandchildren's future. The legacy America gives to Kate, to all children, will ultimately be good, regularly giving them the upbeat outlook on life that a sunny start to a day offers. I know it will be good because there are so many Americans who are just good-hearted, skilled, creative, hardworking, and caring.

The "players" in this book provide lots of positive examples.

The role models, the health care professionals, the salt of the earth Arts and Darlenes, the insightful school kids, and the many who live comprehensively patriotic lives day in and day out. Any one of us can take a couple of newspapers, check out You-tubes, read tweets, or watch a few news casts to come up with a long list of heartwarming stories of the goodness that dominates who Americans are. (America doesn't have a corner on the good people market, but in this book I have focused only on my country.) We have people creating sunny weather forecasts day in and day out. The few specific examples I report below are merely single rays of the sunshine that comes out every day.

Regarding courage and generosity. The guy who spent years perfecting the Minnesota-made pillow went through years of major difficulty. With help of good, skilled people, he came out of those difficult years and turned his life around. He is now paying his thanks forward in such ways as making huge donations to the Salvation Army.

Regarding creative, hardworking, and skilled. I am regularly amazed to hear or read about what people have invented, created, or discovered. A partial list includes electronic and digital stuff galore. New best practices in virtually any aspect of life. Medical devices. Research that produces vehicles with much-improved gas mileage and that pollute less. Driverless cars. Processes that can clean up polluted land and water bodies. Mind-challenging, fascinating games for our handhelds. Creative music styles and artistic mediums. And often new discoveries begin in backyard invention labs. It's easy to believe any challenge the future gives us can be taken on and met.

Regarding displays of empathy and "helping out." We have all seen individuals, sometimes within their faith communities or other organizations, *regularly* caring and providing help to others. They visit people confined to their homes and actively and skillfully help out people who struggle to recover from one or more types of addiction. Kids help by selling lemonade and donating proceeds to local charities; some ask birthday party guests to donate to a charity instead of giving gifts to the birthday kid. People donate to social service organizations that provide free of charge help to those in need. Many roll up their sleeves to prepare food for the hungry, many of whom also need a friend and social interaction. We shift a day's plans in order to shovel driveways and mow lawns for neighbors who can't do it themselves, or we help sort and pack items that go to people in areas of the world and our own nation who are far less well-off than we are.

The ways that so many individuals put a smile on our faces, warm our hearts, give us hope, encourage us, inspire us, put sunshine into our lives to counter the cloudy times we all experience are numerous and varied. My hope is that the spirit in which the goodness is given will inspire us to pass it on to others.

In this book I've asked you to think about the legacy America is giving our kids. I hope you are talking with others because passing on a legacy to all of America's kids requires a *community* level of commitment. It's not an issue of *what* legacy we give them. Legacies happen. By talking about the legacy we *want* to pass on, we evaluate what's going on in America and consciously set goals—for our own family units, our local communities, and ultimately our nation.

This book has looked into many, diverse aspects of American life. I've used a variety of stories to make a conscious effort to point out what is human reality—who we are is influenced by many, many factors. I hope the chapters in this book have brought the *values* you want for our kids to a more conscious place in your mind. I believe each of us can get a clearer picture of how we can better help *all* kids succeed and be happy. The really cool thing about simply getting this clearer picture is that we will naturally, perhaps a bit more consciously, help our families, local communities, and nation be collectively more successful.

Legacies are about values. There are two definitions for *legacy* in my *Webster's New World Dictionary*. The first one is, I guess, what most of us hear about: "money or property left to someone by a will." That's fine. It's a kind and responsible goal to help our kids and grandkids put food on their tables and, perhaps, enjoy certain luxuries they might otherwise not get.

But this book is really about Webster's second definition: "anything handed down from, or as from, an ancestor or predecessor." I want the "anything handed down" from me to be a tool kit that helps my kids and grandkids build happy and successful lives and be able to fix "things" in their lives when fixin' is needed. The tools in my kit that I've used in my life are a mix of what I was given—tools I've received from generously helpful people, and tools I've "purchased" through personal experience.

The tools I'm talking about are the ones I've needed to help me do a lot of important things in my life: get along with other people, solve problems, discover that persistence and hard work pay off, save all kinds of things (including money) for rainy days, learn how important it is to be a good neighbor, participate in making neighborhoods and my country function well, and relax and breathe in the power of nature. I'm not sure how long this list could be!

These and other pieces of the legacy that I want to pass on are all based on the nature and strength of my values and the values of my nation. How I act out each one of the list above can either move me and the world in a good direction or in a bad direction. I can choose to get along with people by trying to force my ideas on them, or I can choose to collaborate with them. I can choose to solve problems by making sure, at whatever cost to others, I get what I want, or I can choose to do unto others what I'd want them to do unto me. My point doesn't need endless examples—*my values determine how I live.* And how I live determines how successful my family, my local communities, and my nation (and world) will be.

If I were to sum up what I want my legacy to do for my kids and grandkids, it would be that they pick up good values; good values lead the way to shaping successful, productive, and happy lives. I can work to pass on good values to my kids and grandkids, but I know that much of what happens in America will collectively be influencing them too. That's why it is so important for all of us to collaborate and work well together.

Appendix

Values are central to our success, as persons and as communities of any size. Each of us has our own major sources of how we came to value what we do, how we obtained the values that guide us. I often think about how the wording and concepts in four documents have affected me, so I've included them for you to consider, perhaps inspiring you to recall your major "values guides" and keep them handy as important reminders. The value guides quoted below influenced why and how I've written this book.

The first values source comes from my religious faith. Christianity's Bible is a practical guide for me. Much of its contents makes sense in how I best relate to other people, how I interact with the physical world, and how I manage the resources I've been given and earned—legacies passed on to me. Since Christianity is so comprehensive, I chose to use one values statement, what we commonly call the Golden Rule.

"So in everything, do to others what you would have them do to you, for this sums up the Law and the Prophets."

MATTHEW 7:12

(The Holy Bible, New International Version,® NIV® Copyright © 1973, 1978, 1984, 2011 by Biblica, Inc.® Used by permission. All rights reserved worldwide.)

The second values guide I was introduced to is the Scout Law of the Boy Scouts of America. I needed to memorize it and, due to periodically restating it, can still say each of the twelve points in order. It is a values guide that was instilled into me as an impressionable kid. It has become a lifelong guide that seven decades of experience have shown me are practical and wise.

<u>The Scout Law</u>

A Scout is **Trustworthy**.

A Scout is **Loyal**.

A Scout is **Helpful**.

A Scout is **Friendly**.

A Scout is **Courteous**.

A Scout is **Kind**.

A Scout is **Obedient**.

A Scout is **Cheerful**.

A Scout is **Thrifty**.

A Scout is **Brave**.

A Scout is **Clean**.

A Scout is **Reverent**.

(The Scout Law is a trademark of the Boy Scouts of America. Used with permission. The Boy Scout Handbook 2016, 13th edition.)

A third values guide comes from my formal education as a student and, later, as a social studies teacher. The Founders of our nation were wise and passionate in wanting to make the nation succeed. The introduction to our constitution, in amazingly few words, sums up what is needed for a nation to succeed. The Preamble was on my mind a lot as I wrote many of the chapters of this book.

Preamble of the Constitution of the United States of America

"We the People of the United States, in Order to form a more perfect Union, establish Justice, insure domestic Tranquility, provide for the common defence, promote the general Welfare, and secure the Blessings of Liberty to ourselves and our Posterity, do ordain and establish this Constitution for the United States of America."

(United States Archives and Records Administration)

Another briefly-worded values guide became a complement to the other three when I joined Rotary International. The organization was formed in 1905 when four Chicago business-men met to discuss how they could promote a friendly spirit among businessmen. The "4 Way Test" was written in 1932 by Rotarian Herbert J. Taylor and now is translated into over 100 languages. I believe it is so highly respected nearly a century later because it makes sense as we think about why good relationships thrive.

<u>The 4 Way Test</u>

"Of the things we think, say or do

Is it the TRUTH?

Is it FAIR to all concerned?

Will it build GOODWILL and better friendships?

Will it be BENEFICIAL to all concerned?"

(Used with permission from The 4 Way Test Association, www.4waytest.org)

About the Author

Jon has lived an experience-rich life. He's taken some hits that have helped him grow and gotten some lucky breaks. Always curious, he's explored life in rural, small town, and big city settings.

Jon is parent to two boys and a girl—good planning, he says, to have Nate and Ben first to help when Meggin got to dating age. Having left the home nest soon after high school, they are leading lives that make parents proud, and have blessed Jon with nine grandchildren. Great memories of "being Dad" remind him of the good feelings from the hanging-out-with-kids experience.

Jon's work history started early. He jumped at the opportunity to work on a potato and grain farm when he finished seventh grade, getting paid a bit for having fun. Nearly six decades of work has given Jon many opportunities to explore the people world and the physical world, and to him work was more of a reward than something you had to do.

Fresh out of college, Jon served kids in Duluth, MN, as a church youth director. That experience, along with summers as a camp counselor in the Black Hills, helped him prepare for relating to kids during his twenty-three-year career as a teacher and ten more years as a secondary school assistant principal.

Bit by the entrepreneurial bug late in life, Jon never retired; instead, he formed a small conflict management LLC. He has also found time to volunteer in a community school, at his church, and with the local chamber of commerce. He served five years on the Bloomington, MN, Planning Commission before being elected to the City Council in 2013.

Jon's life has been supported and guided by his Christian faith. Participating in a faith community is important to him, and he doesn't hesitate to talk about its importance in his life.